I0411213

SSE-100-1

NATIONAL SECURITY AGENCY INFORMATION ASSURANCE GUIDANCE FOR SYSTEMS BASED ON A SECURITY REAL-TIME OPERATING SYSTEM

SYSTEMS SECURITY ENGINEERING

NATIONAL SECURITY AGENCY

9800 SAVAGE ROAD, SUITE 6755

FT. MEADE, MD 20755-6755

IA-GUIDANCE@NSA.GOV

14 DECEMBER 2005

TABLE OF CONTENTS

TABLE OF TABLES

TABLE OF FIGURES

Executive Summary

The emergence of commercial off-the-shelf (COTS) real-time operating systems (RTOS) with the capability to support processing data at multiple classification levels on a single processor while maintaining the necessary data separation has generated significant interest, particularly by embedded system developers. The opportunity to leverage this technology to reduce size, weight and power requirements or to provide more capabilities within an existing footprint drove the need for appropriate Information Assurance (IA) guidance to enable these gains. The National Security Agency (NSA) established a cross-organizational team to develop the necessary IA guidance and this document is the product of that effort. Within this document the term Security Real-Time Operating System (SRTOS) is defined as a separation kernel-based RTOS that has undergone an appropriate security evaluation. Four operational scenarios are described in detail with the intent that any given embedded system would be similar to one of them. For three of the scenarios detailed IA guidance is provided that can be tailored and applied. The IA guidance for the fourth scenario is that it be re-architected because any reasonable IA guidance would not provide sufficient protection to counter the threat. The IA guidance provided in this document addresses many topics including the robustness level of components, layering components, component re-evaluation, use of cache and direct memory access, partitioning, scheduling, communications, devices, covert channel analysis, initialization, life cycle protection measures, and other topics. This IA guidance is targeted at the systems engineers and Information Systems Security Engineers (ISSE) that are developing embedded systems that will be based on a SRTOS and will perform security critical functions such as the separation of data at multiple classification levels. The table below is a summary of the topics and IA guidance. It is provided as an aid to the IA practitioner and a snapshot of the document's content.

SUMMARY OF IA GUIDANCE FOR EMBEDDED SYSTEMS IMPLEMENTING A SECURITY REAL-TIME OPERATING SYSTEM (SRTOS)

Scenario Characteristics	Scenario A	Scenario B	Scenario C	Scenario D
Physical	Low Risk	Low Risk	High Risk	High Risk
User Clearance/Nationality	S, US	U-TS, US and Non-US	U-S, US and non-US	U-TS/SCI, US and non-US
Security Domain Levels	U-S	U-TS	U-S	U-TS/SCI
Network Connectivity	Limited	Limited	NIPRNet+SIPRNet	NIPRNet+SIPRNet+JWICS
Apps/Protocols/Data Types	Limited	Limited	Broad	Broad
IA Guidance				
SRTOS Robustness	Medium Robustness (MR)	High Robustness (HR)	High Robustness (HR)	Not Recommended
Covert Channel Analysis	Not necessary	Systematic with focus on cryptographic data	Systematic	Recommend re-architecting the system so that it is a combination of Scenarios A-C. For an embedded system with JWICS access processing U-TS/SCI data with uncleared users and NIPRNet connectivity the recommended security mechanisms and assurance exceed High Robustness and would likely be impractical.
Privilege Mode	SK/BSP/ASP and as required	Limit to SK/BSP/ASP	Limit to SK/BSP/ASP	
Protection Measures	Blind Buy, Trusted Delivery, Anti-Tamper	Blind Buy, Trusted Delivery, Anti-Tamper	Blind Buy, Trusted Delivery, Anti-Tamper, other measures	
Evaluation	If changes do not affect software, consider penetration testing. If changes affect software do appropriate re-evaluation.			
Secure System Architecture	Address IA threat, apply Information Systems Security Engineering (ISSE), conduct appropriate test/evaluation/analysis			
Partitions	Keep number reasonable, avoid mixing robustness levels within a partition			
Cache	Use is OK if cache was enabled and used during SRTOS evaluation			
DMA	DMA devices need evaluation at SRTOS robustness level			
Scheduling	Ensure security critical functions get necessary resources, not necessarily rigid scheduling of partitions			
Inter-Processor Communications	Enforce Information Flow Control Policy at SRTOS robustness level			
Devices	Single-level Devices and Device Drivers need at least Basic Robustness evaluation. Multi-level Devices and Device Drivers need evaluation at SRTOS robustness level.			
Dynamic Resource Reallocation	Recommended only if SRTOS supports dynamically reallocating resources. Controlling application needs evaluation at SRTOS robustness level.			
Initialization	Ensure system reaches secure state. Clear resources before allocating. Ensure configuration updates done securely.			

Table 1: Summary of IA Guidance

1 BACKGROUND

The Systems Security Engineering organization within the National Security Agency (NSA)/Information Assurance Directorate (IAD) recognized a growing trend in the use and proposed use of commercial Real-Time Operating Systems (RTOS) to perform security critical functions. Multiple system development programs were requesting Information Assurance (IA) guidance for these applications. To ensure that these programs received the highest quality and consistent IA guidance, a decision was made to form a cross-organizational Tiger Team to develop the IA guidance and coordinate it with applicable organizations, thereby providing a source document of IA guidance that could be tailored and applied appropriately to these multiple system development programs.

The RTOS Tiger Team began work in March 2005. Members included:

- John Campbell from Global Information Grid (GIG) Infrastructure Information System Security Engineering (ISSE)

- Vince DiMaria from ISSE for Department of Defense (DoD) Systems (Team Leader)

- Tim Greenwalt from IA Solutions Testing and Integration

- Joyce Lukowski from ISSE for DoD Systems

- Patrick McGeehan from Cross Domain Solutions

- Christopher Pierce from ISSE for DOD Systems

To produce this document, the RTOS Tiger Team met with representatives of programs using or planning to use an RTOS for security critical functions. The team also met with security evaluators and subject matter experts from across NSA/IAD, external organizations, and RTOS vendors.

These programs, evaluators, internal and external organizations, and the vendors provided valuable input and context for the guidance contained in this document. Throughout the process of developing this guidance it became clear that an important topic would have to be addressed by future efforts. This topic is summarized in Section 11. Questions, comments and recommendations about this document may be addressed to:

IA-Guidance@nsa.gov.

2   SCOPE

This document contains system-level IA guidance for embedded systems based on a Security Real-Time Operating System (SRTOS) to provide security critical functions such as the processing of data at differing classification levels. The IA guidance provided is for the overall embedded system, not just the SRTOS itself. The embedded system is an integration of multiple components, some of which perform security critical functions. One of these components is the SRTOS.

To date some systems, primarily aircraft weapon systems, have used custom-developed RTOSs as an IA component within the system processing data at differing classification levels. There is a growing desire and need to use commercial RTOSs that meet certain security requirements to provide security critical functions in a significant number of embedded systems under development. The success of these programs therefore hinges in part on the appropriate application of high quality, consistent IA guidance for these integration activities. It is intended to be applied by ISSEs and other members of the systems engineering team. The document provides definitions for relevant terms and their relationships, explains the characteristics of a "Security RTOS," defines several scenarios reflecting common applications of an SRTOS, provides IA guidance for those scenarios, and provides insight into the policies and regulations that may apply to those scenarios.

3 APPLICABILITY

The intended user of the information contained in this document is the ISSE and other members of the systems engineering team developing a system in which an RTOS will provide security critical functions. The document will likely also be useful to RTOS developers, system evaluators, and system development program offices.

This document is intended to provide IA guidance to the system development effort. Towards that end, it should be studied and applied early in the system development process so as to appropriately affect the system design. As guidance, this document does not specify what is "right" and what is "wrong." That decision is made by the system developer, certifier, and accreditor. In many applications of this guidance a DoD or Intelligence Community body such as the Defense Information Systems Network (DISN) Security Accreditation Working Group (DSAWG), or the Defense Intelligence Community Accreditation Support Team (DICAST) will also play a role in the decision making. That said, rationale for deviating from the guidance should be documented and approved by the appropriate organizations.

The document focuses on providing IA guidance for embedded systems relying on security critical functions implemented, at least in part, by an SRTOS. Embedded systems can use general-purpose operating systems so the guidance may have some applicability to those systems however the guidance assumes the use of an SRTOS. The definition and characteristics of an SRTOS can be found in Section 6.

Within this document, embedded system is used to refer to a combination of hardware and software designed to perform a dedicated function. In most cases, embedded systems are part of a larger system; for example, a Communication/ Navigation/Identification embedded system within an aircraft. An embedded system is a type of information system. Since the IA guidance was developed assuming an embedded system it is necessary to distinguish an embedded system from a general purpose system. Examples of embedded systems range from the embedded system that controls a microwave oven to that controlling a commercial plane. Examples of general purpose Information Technology (IT) systems would range from a typical Personal Computer (PC) to the Internet and Non-Classified Internet Protocol Router Network (NIPRNet). Components within general purpose IT systems could include embedded systems such as the embedded system within a printer that controls its operation. Embedded systems could include components commonly used in general purpose IT systems such as microprocessors and memory and implement some of the same standards such as Transmission Control Protocol/Internet Protocol (TCP/IP). The key difference for the purpose of this document is that an embedded system performs a dedicated function designed into the embedded system by its developer. General purpose systems are designed by their developers to be general purpose, to allow the end user or customer to add, delete, or modify the functions performed by the system. It is the difference between a printer and a PC.

In using this document, read through the first six sections to determine whether or not the guidance will have application to the system you are interested in. Section 7 of the document describes a representative set of operational environment scenarios. Review this section and determine which of the scenarios most closely represents your system. Section 8 and its subsections contain guidance that is specific to each scenario. Rather than reading the entire section, you can go directly to the scenario subsection you are interested in. Please note that Section 8.6 has application to all scenarios and should be reviewed. For information on applicable policy, see Section 9.

4 ASSUMPTIONS AND CONSTRAINTS

This document is based on a number of assumptions and constraints. Those assumptions and constraints are described below and should be reviewed to ensure the IA guidance is appropriate and applied appropriately.

An assumption is made that an RTOS meeting the necessary security requirements and evaluated to a sufficient level of assurance is available as a commercial product from one or more vendors. Basically, the IA guidance assumes the SRTOS is "good" and then proceeds to provide system-level IA guidance on the integration of that SRTOS within an embedded system. The section in this document on the characteristics of an SRTOS further explains what is meant by a "good" SRTOS.

In defining the characteristics of an SRTOS, an assumption was made that appropriate documentation, most likely Protection Profiles (PP), would be developed for the SRTOS and possibly other components, and that the SRTOS and other components were evaluated and found to conform to the approved PPs.

RTOSs are often used in real-time embedded systems. The IA guidance applies to real-time and non-real-time embedded systems but for real-time embedded systems, the IA guidance may need to be altered if there is appropriate justification. The IA guidance assumes the SRTOS is being used to perform, at least in part, a security critical function. Primarily, the scenarios against which the IA guidance was developed use the SRTOS to ensure separation of data at differing classification levels. In these scenarios it was assumed that a poor or incorrect application of the SRTOS could lead to disclosure, modification, or deletion of classified data by a person/process without the necessary authorization and clearance. It is this poor or incorrect application that the IA guidance is intended to address or prevent.

References within this document to "Basic Robustness," "Medium Robustness," and "High Robustness" are based on definitions of these terms in the corresponding "Consistency Instruction Manual for US Government Protection Profiles For Use In Basic Robustness Environments" and the "Consistency Instruction Manual For US Government Protection Profiles for Use In Medium Robustness Environments" available on the National Information Assurance Program (NIAP) Web site. At present, the Consistency Instruction Manual for "High Robustness" is still in draft. Once approved, it will be available on the NIAP Web site. Note that these same terms are given different definitions in IA policies and regulations such as Chairman of the Joint Chiefs of Staff Manual (CJCSM) 6510.01.

The guidance does not consider the IA implications of an SRTOS supporting multiple processors such as in Symmetric Multi-Processing (SMP) or an SRTOS running on a processor with more than a single core (such as dual-core processors). This document applies to systems that may have multiple processors in which the SRTOS runs on each processor and each processor is single core. In addition there is a constraint that the processor hosting the SRTOS must be capable of at least two modes (a privilege mode and a user mode, at a minimum).

Throughout this document the term "privilege mode" refers to a user or process having full access to all resources in a system. It is sometimes referred to as "supervisor mode," "kernel space," or "kernel mode." Throughout this document the terms "system" and "network" are used to refer to systems. For example, the NIPRNet network refers to the entire system (user computers, servers, IA devices, routers, switches, etc), not just a packet routing communications infrastructure.

5 DEFINITIONS

Word	Definition	Source
Assurance	Measure of confidence that the security features, practices, procedures and architecture of an information system accurately mediate and enforce the security policy.	The Committee on National Security Systems (CNSS) Instruction No. 4009, Revised May 2003
Architecture Support Package (ASP)	Software that runs in privilege mode and provides a layer of abstraction between the operating system's kernel and the hardware based on the processor family/architecture (for example PowerPC). Also referred to as the Central Processing Unit (CPU) Support Package.	
Basic Robustness	Security services and mechanisms that equate to good commercial practices. Also see the Consistency Instruction Manual for development of US Government Protection Profiles for use in Basic Robustness Environments on the NIAP Web site.	Department of Defense Directive (DoDD) 8500.1
Board Support Package (BSP)	Software that runs in privilege mode and provides a layer of abstraction between the operating system's kernel and the hardware comprising the computing system.	
Covert Channel	Unintended and/or unauthorized communications path that can be used to transfer information in a manner that violates an information system's security policy.	CNSS Instruction No. 4009, Revised May 2003
Cross Domain Solutions	An information assurance solution that provides the ability to manually and/or automatically access and/or transfer data between two or more differing security domains.	CJCSI 6211.02B, 31 July 2003
Evaluation Assurance Level (EAL)	A set of assurance requirements that represent a point on the Common Criteria predefined assurance scale.	CNSS Instruction No. 4009, Revised May 2003
Embedded System	A combination of hardware and software designed to perform a dedicated function. In most cases, embedded systems are part of a larger system such as the Communication/Navigation/Identification embedded system within an aircraft.	
Filter	A security policy enforcement mechanism that mediates cross-domain data flows to safeguard against the improper release of sensitive information and the infiltration of malicious content.	

Word	Definition	Source
Guard	Mechanism limiting the exchange of information between systems (CNSSI 4009, May 2003). A guard is a class or type of cross domain solution that mediates the flow of information between or among differing security domains. The primary functions of a guard are to protect against the unauthorized disclosure of information and the infiltration of malicious content (eg., viruses, trojans, executable code). Also referred to as a cross domain guard.	CNSS Instruction No. 4009, Revised May 2003
High Robustness	The security services and mechanisms that provide the most stringent protection and rigorous security countermeasures.	www.iatf.net appendix E
Information Flow Control	A procedure to ensure that information transfers within a system are only made if permitted by the system's security policy.	
Medium Robustness	Security Services and mechanisms that provide for layering of additional safeguards above good commercial practices. Also see the Consistency Instruction Manual for development of US Government Protection Profiles for use in Medium Robustness Environments on the NIAP Web site.	DoDD 8500.1
Partition	A set of subjects and a set of exported resources that are within the same policy-based equivalence class as defined by the configuration data. For a given partition, either but not both sets may be empty. Resources that are by default accessible by all partitions are virtualized and exported. The configuration data assigns (binds) each exported resource to a single partition for the purposes of defining such partitions. Every subject is assigned (bound) to a single partition by the configuration data for the purposes of defining partitions.	Draft US Government Protection Profile for Separation Kernels in Environments Requiring High Robustness
Privilege Mode	An operational state of hardware or software that has the broadest permission set, unconstrained access to resources. Also called the "kernel space," "kernel mode," "supervisor mode," or "supervisor state," it is typically the mode in which the operating system runs.	
Protection Profile	Common Criteria specification that represents an implementation-independent set of security requirements for a category of Target of Evaluations that meets specific consumer needs.	CNSS Instruction No. 4009, Revised May 2003

Word	Definition	Source
Real-Time Operating System	Operating systems implementing components and services that explicitly offer deterministic responses.	
Security RTOS	An SRTOS is a separation kernel-based Real Time Operating System that has undergone an appropriate security evaluation.	
Separation Kernel	A hardware and/or firmware mechanism whose primary function is to separate multiple partitions and control information flow between and within the partitions.	Draft US Government Protection Profile for Separation Kernels in Environments Requiring High Robustness
Separation Kernel Protection Profile (SKPP) (Based on CC ver 2.2)	Specifies the security functional and assurance requirements for a class of separation kernels. Unlike the traditional security kernel that performs all trusted functions for a secure operating system, a separation kernel's primary security function is to partition the subjects and resources of a system into policy-based equivalence classes, and to control information flows between partitions. See "Separation Kernel" and "Protection Profile".	http://niap.nist.gov/pp/draft_pps /pp_draft_skpp_hr_v0.621.html
Target of Evaluation	IT product or system and its associated administrator and user guidance documentation that is the subject of an evaluation.	CNSS Instruction No. 4009, Revised May 2003
Threat	Any circumstance or event with the potential to adversely impact an Information System (IS) through unauthorized access, destruction, disclosure, modification of data, and/or denial of service.	CNSS Instruction No. 4009, Revised May 2003

Table 2: Definitions

6 SECURITY RTOS CHARACTERISTICS

6.1 SRTOS DEFINITION AND CHARACTERISTICS

An SRTOS is a separation kernel-based Real Time Operating System that has undergone an appropriate security evaluation.

The SRTOS definition states that one characteristic of an SRTOS is that it is a Real Time Operating System (RTOS). An RTOS is an operating system implementing components and services that explicitly offer deterministic responses, and therefore allow the creation of hard real-time systems. Typical applications of an RTOS are embedded systems with real time requirements. Real time requirements are often characterized as situations where the consequences of receiving data late are the same as not receiving the data at all. An example would be a fighter plane's need to release chaff within X milliseconds of detecting an incoming missile. A late command has the same consequence as no command in this situation.

The SRTOS definition states that the SRTOS is separation kernel-based. A separation kernel is a mechanism whose primary function is to separate multiple partitions and control information flow between the partitions. It provides time and space partitioning and information flow control.

Figure 1 illustrates an SRTOS performing time and space partitioning. At any given time a single partition is active, such as partition A on the left side of the figure, and software within that partition is executed by the processor and can access resources (for example memory) as depicted by the A square in the figure. Note that the B and C squares shown within the A partition on the left side of the figure represent resources belonging to partitions B and C, respectively, and they are grayed-out signifying that these resources are unavailable to partition A (processes running within partition A). After a designated period of time, or in response to some control input, the SRTOS performs a context switch and partition B becomes the active partition. The context switch performed by the SRTOS involves saving the state of the processor for partition A, under the control of the SRTOS, and setting the state of the processor to the previously saved state for partition B. Since partition B is now the active partition it can continue executing from wherever it left off when a previous context switch was made. Partition B will execute and have access to the B resources (but not A or C resources) until the SRTOS performs a context switch and partition C becomes active.

13

The phrase "time and space partitioning" can be broken down into "time partitioning" and "space partitioning." Time partitioning refers to how the SRTOS can ensure that only one partition is active at any given time, thus dividing/partitioning time between partitions A, B and C in the figure. Space partitioning refers to the address space available to the SRTOS and represents all the resources available to the SRTOS. The address space is depicted in the figure by the small rectangle, subdivided into squares representing the portion of address space allocated to partition A, the portion of address space allocated to partition B, and likewise for partition C. The SRTOS then provides space partitioning by ensuring that partition A only has access to the portion/partition of address space allocated to partition A and not to address space allocated to partitions B or C.

The SRTOS also enforces information flow control. In many cases there will be requirements for some data to be shared by multiple partitions. An SRTOS can accomplish this in a variety of ways. One way is to allocate a portion of address space to multiple partitions. For example, if a portion of the total address space is allocated to partitions A and B then when partition A is active it could store data in that address space (memory) and when partition B becomes active it could read data from that address space. In this example, the SRTOS is enforcing the flow of information between partitions A, B and C by allowing the flow of information between partitions A and B but preventing any flow of information between partitions A and C or between partitions B and C.

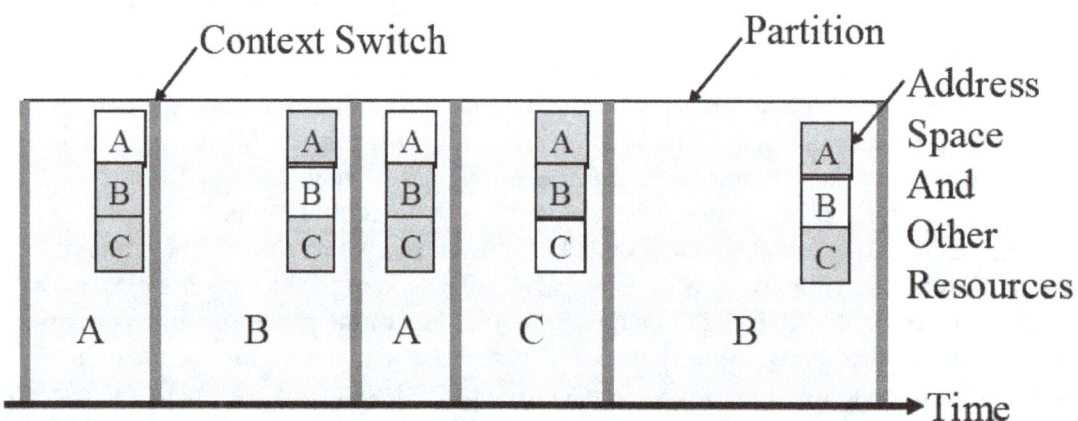

Context Switch – SRTOS takes control from Partition A, saves processor state A, restores processor state B, passes control to Partition B (takes <1 msec)

Figure 1: SRTOS Time and Space Partitioning

The SRTOS definition states that the SRTOS has undergone an appropriate security evaluation. Section 8.6 of this document addresses IA guidance for several scenarios and recommends the use of a Medium Robustness SRTOS or High Robustness SRTOS, depending on the scenario and a variety of factors.

A Medium Robustness SRTOS should be evaluated against a Security Target that conforms to a US Government Protection Profile (PP) that adequately addresses the security mechanisms required by that SRTOS to perform its intended functions. The PP should comply with the Consistency Instruction Manual for US Government Protection Profiles for Medium Robustness Environments. The PP would, as a starting point, use the security requirements from the US Government Protection Profile for Separation Kernels in Environments Requiring High Robustness (SKPP) and the assurance requirements from the US Government Protection Profile for Multilevel Operating System in Environments Requiring Medium Robustness.

A High Robustness SRTOS should be evaluated against a Security Target that conforms to the SKPP. The SRTOS should, as a minimum, provide all the capabilities described in the SKPP. These include the ability to manage partitions (including partitioning and scheduling) and to ensure that any information flow between partitions is expressly permitted by a security policy enforced by the SRTOS.

While the above describes the minimum characteristics of an SRTOS it is likely that any particular SRTOS will include additional features and capabilities. For example, an SRTOS may include the ability to verify the integrity and source of the software in a particular partition. All features and capabilities of the SRTOS should be addressed in the SRTOS Security Target. The key criteria in determining whether something is part of the SRTOS or not is whether that software will execute in privilege mode. Any software that executes in privilege mode is considered to be part of the SRTOS. "Privilege mode" is used throughout this document and should be considered to have the same meaning as kernel space, ring 0, or supervisory mode.

6.2   RELATIONSHIP BETWEEN 178B RTOS AND SRTOS

The Federal Aviation Administration's (FAA) Advisory Circular AC20-115B identifies DO-178B, Software Considerations in Airborne Systems and Equipment Certification, as one possible means for obtaining FAA approval of aviation software. DO-178B is a standard developed and maintained by RTCA Inc. that requires strong configuration management, detailed documentation, a rigorous development process, etc, to ensure flight safety. It is possible that an SRTOS would need to conform to DO-178B when the SRTOS is considered to be aviation software. However, an SRTOS does not need to be certified as compliant with DO-178B to satisfy the definition of an SRTOS and there are many applications where the SRTOS would not need to conform to DO-178B. Note that conforming to DO-178B does not satisfy the "undergone an appropriate security evaluation" characteristic for an SRTOS stated in the SRTOS definition.

7 ENVIRONMENT SCENARIOS

The following environment scenarios represent typical embedded systems that would use an SRTOS. Each scenario is based on characteristics that define the system's environment. While these are representative of systems, each environment scenario can be tailored to fit the needs for a unique system. The guidance for the unique system would be tailored appropriately.

This section is divided into the characteristics that define the environment scenarios and the descriptions of the environment scenarios.

7.1 CHARACTERISTICS

This section addresses six characteristics of environment scenarios that the guidance applies to, which are: Physical Security, Types of Users, Security Domain Levels, Network Connectivity, Applications, and Protocols and Data Types.

7.1.1 Physical Security

For the purpose of this document, physical security describes the controls and mechanisms in place to protect the system from unauthorized physical access. The properties of these controls and mechanisms could include the operating environment, armed guards, access controls to the system, alarms, property controls and access controls to the system's utilities. The greater number and more effectively these properties are applied, the better the physical security.

Physical security that represents a high risk to the system is characterized by an environment that places the system at significant risk of access by unauthorized personnel. Typical examples would be tactical systems operating in an environment with a significant risk of overrun by an adversary.

Physical security that represents a low risk to the system is characterized by an environment that places the system at minimal risk of access by unauthorized personnel. Typical examples would be systems operating in an environment protected by armed guards and dogs.

Note that whether a system may be subject to physical harm due to combat does not factor into the concept of physical security as it is used in this document.

7.1.2 Types of Users

The embedded system could have many different types of users. The users could be both United States (US) and non-US users. The clearance level of a user could be from uncleared to cleared for access to Top Secret (TS)/Sensitive Compartmented Information (SCI) information.

Some users are 'local' or 'direct' users, accessing and working on the embedded system itself. Users can also be 'remote,' or 'indirect,' in which case their access to the embedded system is via an interface from their own system. Receipt of data from another system is a characteristic of a remote/indirect user.

7.1.3   Security Domain Levels

This characteristic represents the range of classification level of the data processed by the embedded system.   Data in the system could range from Unclassified up to TS/ SCI. Different combinations could include Unclassified through Secret (S)/Special Access Required (SAR) or Secret to Top Secret.

7.1.4   Network Connectivity

Network Connectivity describes the possible types of networks to which the embedded system would be connected. Having connectivity implies that information can flow between an external network, such as the Secret Internet Protocol Router Network (SIPRNet), and the embedded system via a direct connection. In the case of an unclassified embedded system connected directly to the NIPRNet where an external cross domain guard such as a Radiant Mercury transfers data to the SIPRNet, the embedded system would be directly connected to the NIPRNet and Internet and indirectly connected to the SIPRNet. Please note that for this document, network connectivity is used to refer to direct connections only and assumes indirect connections are mediated by an IA mechanism/device external to the embedded system (the Radiant Mercury guard in this example).

In this document, network connectivity to the embedded system is looked at as being broad or limited. Broad connectivity refers to connections/communications with systems where the connectivity has unrestricted functionality and represents a significant threat to the system. Broad connections could also have possibly less network safeguards allowing for a less restricted interface between the embedded system and the network. A broad connection could provide an adversary with a significant opportunity to subvert the system. A connection to the NIPRNet would be an example of broad connectivity. Limited connectivity refers to connections/communications with networks where the connectivity has limited functionality and represents a less significant threat to the embedded system. In limited connectivity, network safeguards could be tightened down to restrict the amount of communication between the network and the embedded system. A limited connection would provide an adversary with a less significant opportunity to subvert the system. A connection to the Global Positioning System (GPS) would be an example of limited connectivity because it is only used for one function. Network connections considered broad would include connections such as SIPRNet, Joint Worldwide Intelligence Communications System (JWICS), coalition networks, NIPRNet, and/or the Internet.

7.1.5   Applications

Within this document "application" refers to the software executing within a partition. It includes typical application software such as a Web browser, but also any other software (for example a device driver, a file system, etc) within a partition.

Each scenario could have applications with either limited or broad functionality. Broad applications are more commonly found and used more often. Broad applications are non-customized and unmodified. Broad applications could also have hidden features. Examples of broad applications are applications such as a word processor or a Web browser. Limited applications are less commonly used and may be custom or unique applications. They are developed in-house or put on contract to be developed. The applications are specifically developed to handle a certain set of tasks. This means that fewer hidden features would likely exist. If the limited application is built to mimic or extend an existing broad application, some features can now be restricted. Limited applications could also be easier to maintain and extend for future development. An example of a limited application is a flight control application in an air vehicle.

While all applications contain vulnerabilities and risk, some contain more than others. Broad applications could represent a higher risk because the applications are more widely used and could have more widely known vulnerabilities. Exploitable hidden features could also become known, creating a new risk. Limited applications could represent lower risk because the applications are less widely used or known, making the vulnerabilities to the limited applications possibly less well known. Also, limited applications have a limited set of features, leaving fewer features to be exploited.

7.1.6 Protocols and Data Types

Protocols could either be broad or limited. A broad protocol is a protocol that is more commonly found and used more often. The broad protocol is non-customized and unmodified. The broad protocol may have hidden features. Examples of broad protocols are TCP/IP or Hypertext Transfer Protocol (HTTP). A limited protocol is a less commonly used protocol that is sometimes custom-created to work specifically for a system. The limited protocols are developed in-house or put on contract to be developed. This means that less hidden features could exist. If the limited protocol is built to mimic or extend an existing broad protocol, some features can now be restricted. Limited protocols could also be easier to maintain and extend for future development.

Choice of protocols is important since they may introduce vulnerabilities. Broad protocols could represent a higher risk because the protocols are more widely used and could have more widely known vulnerabilities. Exploitable hidden features could also become known, creating a new risk. Limited protocols could represent lower risk because the protocols are less widely used or known, making the vulnerabilities to the limited protocols possibly less well known. Also, limited protocols could have a limited set of features, leaving fewer features to be exploited.

Along with protocols, the data types the protocol handles must be taken into account. The data type is the format of the data the protocol uses. The format could be fixed (where information fields are known, e.g. a tactical message or GPS message) or open (e.g. a word document, HTTP Web-based e-mail, American Standard Code for Information Interchange [ASCII] text files, and imagery). Fixed format communication could provide a level of threat mitigation because of the limited set of allowed information fields.

7.2   DESCRIPTION OF ENVIRONMENT SCENARIOS

The following environment scenarios use various combinations of the characteristics defined above. Each scenario is representative of a DoD embedded system that uses an SRTOS. While the scenarios are reflective of a particular system, they can be applied to various systems and modified criteria as needed. When any of the characteristics of the scenario are changed, the other characteristics of the scenario should be examined to see if they have been affected and need adjustment.

7.2.1   Scenario A

Scenario A is an embedded system using multiple processors. An example implementation for Scenario A would be an airborne fighter plane, with limited or no network connections and a predefined flight plan, with limited applications.

Listed below are descriptions of the characteristics of the system environment.

SCENARIO A		
Physical Security	Low Risk	The system exhibits low risk physical security. This could be an air combat vehicle with a low threat of physical tampering while airborne, and physically protected while on the ground, with only cleared individuals accessing the system. As mentioned earlier, physical harm due to combat does not factor into the concept of physical security as it is used in this document.
Types of Users	US S	The users are limited to US citizens. Only cleared individuals access the system.
Security Domain Levels	U-S	The system processes information at Unclassified through Secret levels on a single processor.
Network Connectivity	Limited	The system does not have connections to any major networks such as NIPRNet. The system may have limited connections to external systems for the exchange of data such as GPS. These connections may be at the Secret or Unclassified level.
Applications	Limited	Applications are limited to custom or proprietary applications. The system will use custom applications to read/write messages.
Protocols and Data Types	Limited Fixed	The system will use a limited, custom-made network protocol to transfer messages. The system will use fixed formatted data such as that used with GPS.

7.2.2 Scenario B

Scenario B is an embedded system using multiple processors. An example implementation for Scenario B would be an airborne fighter plane, with limited to no network connections and a predefined flight plan, with limited applications.

Listed below are descriptions of the characteristics of the system environment.

SCENARIO B		
Physical Security	Low Risk	This could be an air combat vehicle with a low threat of physical tampering while airborne, and physically protected while on the ground. As mentioned earlier, physical harm due to combat does not factor into the concept of physical security as it is used in this document.
Types of Users	US & Non-US Uncleared - TS	Users are US citizens as well as foreign allies such as the United Kingdom (UK). The clearance level of the users will vary from uncleared to Top Secret.
Security Domain Levels	U-TS	The system processes information at the Unclassified through Top Secret levels on a single processor.
Network Connectivity	Limited	The system does not have connections to any major networks such as NIPRNet. The system may have limited connections to external systems for the exchange of data such as GPS. These connections may be at the Top Secret, Secret or Unclassified level.
Applications	Limited	Applications are limited to custom or proprietary applications. The system will use custom applications to read/write messages.
Protocols and Data Types	Limited Fixed	The system will use a limited, custom-made network protocol to transfer messages. The system will use fixed formatted data such as that used with GPS.

Table 4: Scenario B

7.2.3 Scenario C

Scenario C is an embedded system using multiple processors. An example implementation for Scenario C would be a ground vehicle, with broad network connections, and with broad applications.

Listed below are descriptions of the characteristics of the system environment.

SCENARIO C		
Physical Security	High Risk	This could be a ground combat vehicle. Because of the potential physical access to the system by unauthorized users, including Non-US users, the system is considered a high-risk environment. As mentioned earlier, physical harm due to combat does not factor into the concept of physical security as it is used in this document.
Types of Users	US & Non-US Uncleared - S	The users of this system will be both US and non-US. The clearance level of the users will vary from uncleared to Secret.
Security Domain Levels	U-S	The system can process information ranging from U to S on a single processor.
Network Connectivity	Broad	The system has broad connections to the NIPRNet and the SIPRNet. The NIPRNet provides connectivity to the Internet.
Applications	Broad	Within the partitions on a processor run broad applications. Applications may include logging and auditing applications, access control applications, office applications, Internet applications like e-mail and a browser, and network intrusion and filtering applications.
Protocols and Data Types	Broad Open	The system will use a broad or commonly used network protocol to transfer the messages, such as TCP/IP. The messages sent will be in an open format.

Table 5: Scenario C

7.2.4 Scenario D

Scenario D is an embedded system using multiple processors. An example implementation for Scenario D would be a ground vehicle, with broad network connections, and with broad applications.

Listed below are descriptions of the characteristics of the system environment.

SCENARIO D		
Physical Security	High Risk	This could be a ground combat vehicle. Because of the potential physical access to the system by unauthorized users, including Non-US users, the system is considered a high-risk environment. As mentioned earlier, physical harm due to combat does not factor into the concept of physical security as it is used in this document.
Types of Users	US & Non-US Uncleared – TS/SCI	The system contains US and Non-US users. The clearance level of the users will vary from uncleared to TS/SCI.

22

Security Domain Levels	U-TS/SCI	The system can process information ranging from Unclassified (U) to TS/SCI on a single processor.
Network Connectivity	Broad	Broad connections to the system include NIPRNet, SIPRNet, and JWICS. The NIPRNet connection connects to the Internet.
Applications	Broad	Applications may include logging and auditing applications, access control applications, office applications, Internet applications like e-mail and a browser, and network intrusion and filtering applications.
Protocols and Data Types	Broad Open	The system will use a broad or commonly used network protocol to transfer the messages, such as TCP/IP. The messages sent will be in an open format.

Table 6: Scenario D

7.3 SUMMARY OF SCENARIOS

The following table summarizes the Scenarios and their characteristics.

SCENARIO	A	B	C	D
Physical Security	Low Risk	Low Risk	High Risk	High Risk
Types of Users	US S	US & Non-US Uncleared-TS	US & Non-US Uncleared-S	US & Non-US Uncleared-TS/SCI
Security Domain Levels	U-S	U-TS	U-S	U-TS/SCI
Network Connectivity	Limited	Limited	Broad	Broad
Applications	Limited	Limited	Broad	Broad
Protocols and Data Types	Limited Fixed	Limited Fixed	Broad Open	Broad Open

Table 7: Environment Scenarios Summary

8 IA GUIDANCE

8.1 INTRODUCTION

This section of the document provides IA guidance for each of the scenarios defined in Section 7. In addition to the guidance for a particular scenario, there is guidance that applies to all scenarios in Section 8.6.

Some systems may contain subsystems where the subsystems each reflect a different scenario. As a starting point, each subsystem should examine the guidance from the scenario that is the closest match. An analysis should then be done to determine if any of the more stringent guidance for one subsystem should be applied to another subsystem in order to ensure the security of the overall system. In many cases relationships between the subsystems will cause the more stringent guidance to apply. It is important that the security afforded to one subsystem by the more stringent guidance is not undercut by applying less stringent guidance to another subsystem.

8.2 IA GUIDANCE FOR SCENARIO A

8.2.1 Description of Scenario A

As described in the Environment Scenario section of this report, Scenario A reflects a system having the general characteristics summarized below:

- Physical Security: Security provided by the physical environment of the system is characterized as low risk. For example, the system is in a physically secure facility or it is protected as classified.

- Types of Users: The system has users within the system that are cleared Secret. No users are uncleared. All users are US citizens.

- Security Domain Levels: The system processes Unclassified and Secret data on a single processor.

- Network Connectivity: The system is not connected to any significant external networks/systems, which would allow large numbers of remote people and processes any degree of access to the system. For example, the system may receive location data from a GPS receiver but it is not connected to the NIPRNet.

- Applications: The applications are limited. An example of a limited application is one that takes in data from a speedometer and adjusts a vehicle's throttle to maintain a constant speed.

24

- Protocols and Data Types: The system has limited protocols that are not in wide use and do not have known vulnerabilities published in open forums. For example, the system may use a customized protocol for communications, designed to only work within that system. The data types implement fixed format messages, such as GPS messages.

8.2.2 Analysis of Scenario A

Primary areas of risk for Scenario A described above include:

- Physical Security: The risk of unauthorized access that could jeopardize the security of the system is minimal because the system is in a physically secure facility and/or protected as classified Secret.

- Types of Users: There is an insider risk posed by the US Secret cleared user. This risk may be minimal since the user is cleared for all information processed by the system.

- Security Domain Levels: As the system processes data only at the Secret and Unclassified levels the value of the data is lower than the value of Top Secret data and an adversary would apply fewer resources towards compromising the data.

- Network Connectivity: There is a risk posed by the connections to external networks/systems. This risk will vary and requires examination of each connection to include the trust level of the user/process at the other end of the connection and the likelihood that information from that user/process could subvert the system. Since Scenario A has limited network connectivity the ability of an adversary to use this connectivity to access and attack the system is likewise limited and hence the risk is low.

- Applications, Protocols and Data Types: The system has limited applications and protocols that are not in wide use and fixed data types and do not have known vulnerabilities published in open forums; therefore the risk from these sources is considered low. This does not mean that one might achieve *security through obscurity* rather than from sound security engineering. Nor should one come to the conclusion that obscure software would permit security critical functions to be performed by low robustness software. Limited applications, data types, and protocols require an adversary to expend resources to obtain the necessary information and discover vulnerabilities. In the case of broad applications, data types, and protocols the information is readily known and vulnerabilities have already been discovered and published, and therefore represent no cost to the adversary.

8.2.3 Example Scenario A System

An example system based on the characteristics of Scenario A is defined below and depicted in Figure 2. The example system provides Secret cleared US users with fused situational awareness using data from within the system and some external input. The system includes a subsystem that can detect certain threats to the platform and respond with countermeasures.

Note that this is only an example of a system that would be consistent with the characteristics for Scenario A. The example system depicted here is only used to illustrate the IA guidance that would be appropriate for any system consistent with the characteristics for Scenario A.

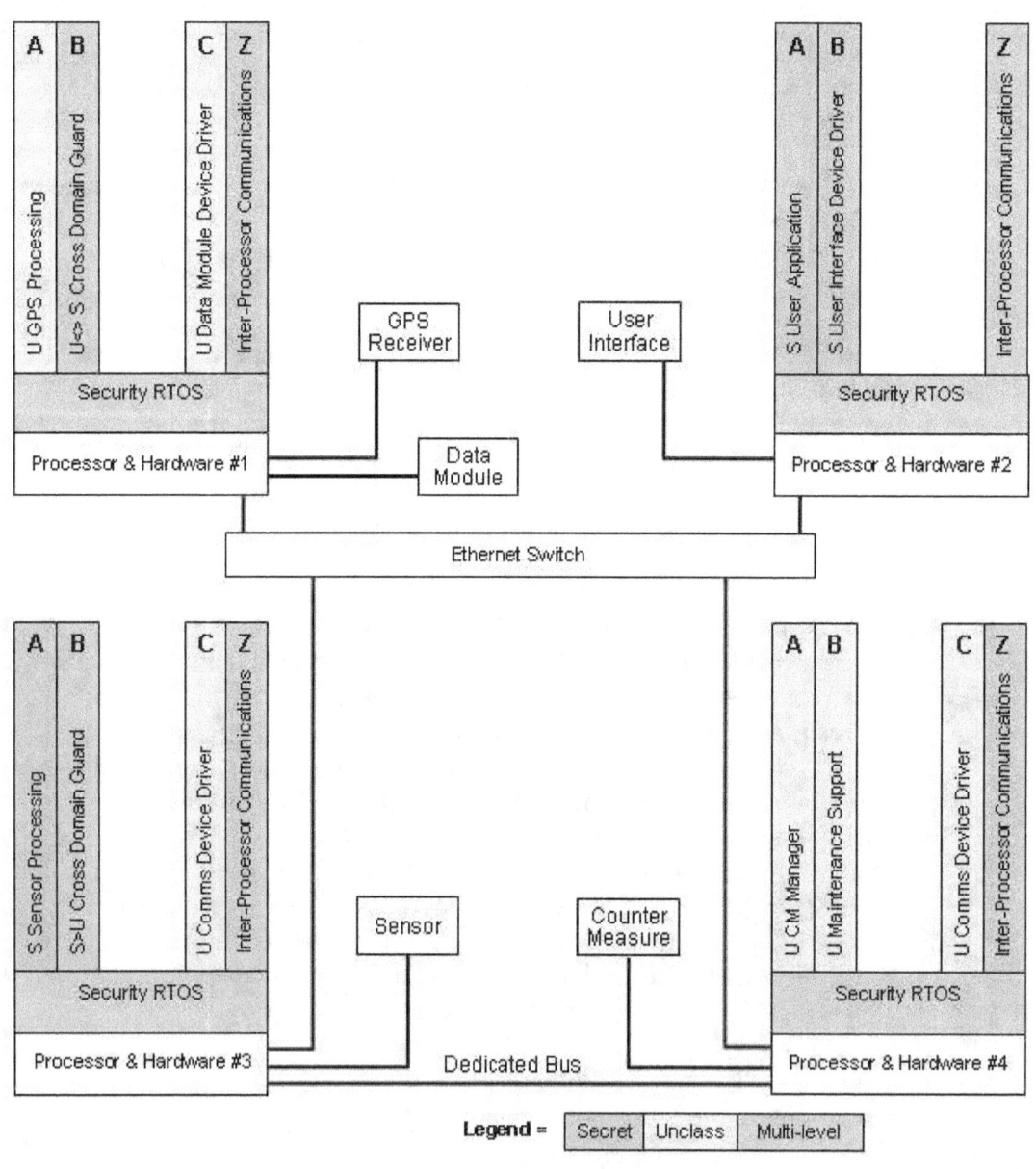

Figure 2: Scenario A

8.2.3.1 COMPONENT DESCRIPTIONS

The following paragraphs describe each of the components in the example system for Scenario A, as depicted in Figure 2. Partitions are represented by the vertical rectangles in the figure, such as "U GPS Processing." A shorthand notation for referring to a particular partition is used in this document. The shorthand notation is the number for the "Processor & Hardware" hosting the partition and the letter shown in the figure for that partition. For example, U Maintenance Support is a partition on Processor & Hardware #4 and is labeled B, so its shorthand notation is 4B. If a partition involves data and processing at a single classification level then that level is included at the beginning of the name of that partition. For example, the "U" in U GPS Processing (1A) indicates that this partition only processes unclassified data. Partitions that support the movement of data between a partition at one classification level and a partition at a different classification level have two classification levels at the beginning of their name, as well as symbols to denote the direction in which the information flows. For example, the S>U Cross Domain Guard (3B) partition supports the movement of data between a Secret partition (S) and an Unclassified partition (U) with the information flowing from the Secret partition to the Unclassified partition (S>U). If information flows in both directions between the partitions "<>" is used, such as in U<>S Cross Domain Guard (1B).

Processor & Hardware represents the hardware components such as microprocessor, memory (volatile and non-volatile), interface devices, etc. This example system is based on four sets of hardware. This illustrates that most systems will have multiple processors and keeps the number of partitions on any one processor to a reasonable number for discussion. Note that the hardware could be the same for all four sets, but that would require that each set of hardware have all of the necessary interfaces. In particular: Processor & Hardware #1 requires a network interface (connection to the Ethernet Switch), a Data Module interface and a GPS Receiver interface; Processor & Hardware #2 requires one network interface and an interface to the User Interface device (perhaps a touch screen display); Processor & Hardware #3 requires one network interface, a Dedicated Bus interface and an interface to the Sensor; and Processor & Hardware #4 requires one network interface, a Dedicated Bus interface and an interface to the Countermeasure.

GPS Receiver represents a device connected to Processor & Hardware #1 that provides unclassified current location information to the system.

Data Module represents a device connected to Processor & Hardware #1 that provides data storage as a means for bringing unclassified data into the system and taking unclassified data away from the system. It represents a removable memory device.

User Interface represents a Secret device connected to Processor & Hardware #2 that provides a means for the user to interact with the system. It displays Secret situational awareness information to the user and it allows the user to enter Secret information for composing situational awareness.

Ethernet Switch represents a device that interconnects the four Processor & Hardware components to allow the exchange of unclassified and Secret data packets. The Ethernet switch just transfers the packets, and the only decisions it makes are related to the delivery of packets.

Sensor represents a device that monitors the surroundings of the system. It passes Secret information concerning anything it detects to the S Sensor Processing (3A) partition for analysis.

Countermeasure represents a device that deploys a countermeasure to protect the system from a threat detected by the Sensor. It is controlled by the U CM Manager (4A) partition.

Security RTOS represents the SRTOS that fulfills all the characteristics of an SRTOS as described in Section 6, Characteristics of a Security RTOS. It is all the software running in privilege mode on a processor. All other software exists in a partition. Each SRTOS enforces a policy that can control:

- what resources (memory, addresses, etc) are available to a partition (space partitioning)

- the amount of time or processor cycles provided to a partition (time partitioning)

- for a given partition, what other partitions on that processor the given partition can pass information to or receive information from (information flow control).

For example, partition 1A, U GPS Processing, would be allocated by the SRTOS on Processor & Hardware #1 a portion of the memory/address space available to the processor/SRTOS that would be sufficient for software running in the U GPS Processing partition. Partition 1A would also be allocated the address(es) necessary for accessing the GPS Receiver interface via Processor & Hardware #1. Partition 1A would be allocated a portion of the available processor cycles. Partition 1A would be allowed to receive information from the GPS Receiver and send information to partition 1B, U⬦S Cross Domain Guard.

U GPS Processing (1A) represents a partition running at the unclassified level that controls the GPS Receiver device and receives position location data from the GPS Receiver. The current location of the system is used within other partitions to provide the user with situational awareness based on the user's current position and input from sensors, etc.

U<>S Cross Domain Guard (1B) represents a partition that performs a cross domain data transfer function. One action is that it takes in unclassified GPS data from the U GPS Processing (1A) partition, checks its format, etc, to determine the data is safe and then passes the data to the Secret S User Application (2A) partition so that the data can be used in providing situational awareness to the user. A second action is that it takes in reporting data from the S User Application (2A) partition, verifies the data is unclassified, etc, and then passes the data to the unclassified Data Module. At a later time the Data Module is removed from the system and the reporting data is placed in another system for analysis.

U Data Module Device Driver (1C) represents a partition running at the unclassified level that handles the interface to the Data Module device. It communicates with the unclassified Data Module via Processor & Hardware #1 and takes care of formatting data for storage on the Data Module.

S User Application (2A) represents a partition running at the Secret level that takes in data from several sources, including the GPS Receiver, Sensor, Data Module and user, and fuses/composes a Secret situational awareness picture for the user. It also creates unclassified reports for storage on the Data Module to be extracted and analyzed at a later time.

S User Interface Device Driver (2B) represents a partition running at the Secret level that handles the interface to the User Interface. It communicates with the User Interface via Processor & Hardware #2.

Inter-Processor Communications (1Z, 2Z, 3Z, and 4Z) is described in Section 8.6.7. In summary, the four Inter-Processor Communications partitions connect via their respective Processor & Hardware to an Ethernet Switch that they share in common. These partitions support communication between partitions on different processors. Each of the four enforces its own security policy, which are subsets of the overall system security policy. For example, the Inter-Processor Communications (1Z) partition on Processor & Hardware #1 will allow partition S User Application (2A) to communicate with partition U<>S Cross Domain Guard (1B) but would not allow S User Application (2A) to communicate with partition U Data Module Device Driver (1C).

S Sensor Processing (3A) represents a partition running at the Secret level that takes in Secret data from the Sensor device and analyzes that data. If S Sensor Processing (3A) detects an immediate threat to the system (perhaps a missile coming towards a fighter plane) then it can initiate an action to respond with a Countermeasure (perhaps releasing chaff from the fighter plane to confuse the missile). S Sensor Processing (3A) also provides its Secret analysis of the data from the Sensor device to the partition S User Application (2A) where that data is used to compose the Secret situational awareness for the user.

S>U Cross Domain Guard (3B) represents a partition that performs a cross domain data transfer function. It takes in a command to respond with a Countermeasure from the partition S Sensor Processing (3A), verifies the data is unclassified, etc, and then passes the command to U CM Manager (4A).

U Comms Device Driver (3C and 4C) represents a partition running at the unclassified level that handles the interface to the Dedicated Bus. This partition exists separately on both Processor & Hardware #3 and Processor & Hardware #4.

Dedicated Bus represents a dedicated serial data bus that transfers information from Processor & Hardware #3 to Processor & Hardware #4. It is used to transfer the command to initiate a Countermeasure from Processor & Hardware #3 to Processor & Hardware #4. The Dedicated Bus interface on Processor & Hardware #3 can only be accessed by the U Comms Device Driver (3C) partition, a policy enforced by the SRTOS. The Dedicated Bus interface on Processor & Hardware #4 can only be accessed by the U Comms Device Driver (4C) partition, a policy enforced by the SRTOS.

U CM Manager (4A) represents a partition running at the unclassified level that controls the Countermeasure device and tracks usage of the Countermeasure. It reports usage of the Countermeasure to the U Maintenance Support (4B) partition.

U Maintenance Support (4B) represents a partition running at the unclassified level that receives information on the expenditure of Countermeasures and tracks Countermeasure usage. When replenishment of the Countermeasure is necessary the U Maintenance Support (4B) partition can store this unclassified fact in the Data Module. After a mission when the data in the Data Module is analyzed the need to replenish the supply of Countermeasures within the system will be recognized.

8.2.3.2 DETECT AND RESPOND

If processing/analyzing of sensor data identifies an immediate threat then S Sensor Processing (3A) sends a command to initiate an appropriate countermeasure (CM) to the U CM Manager (4A). Since the command is originating in an S partition and going to a U partition it must pass through a Cross Domain Guard.

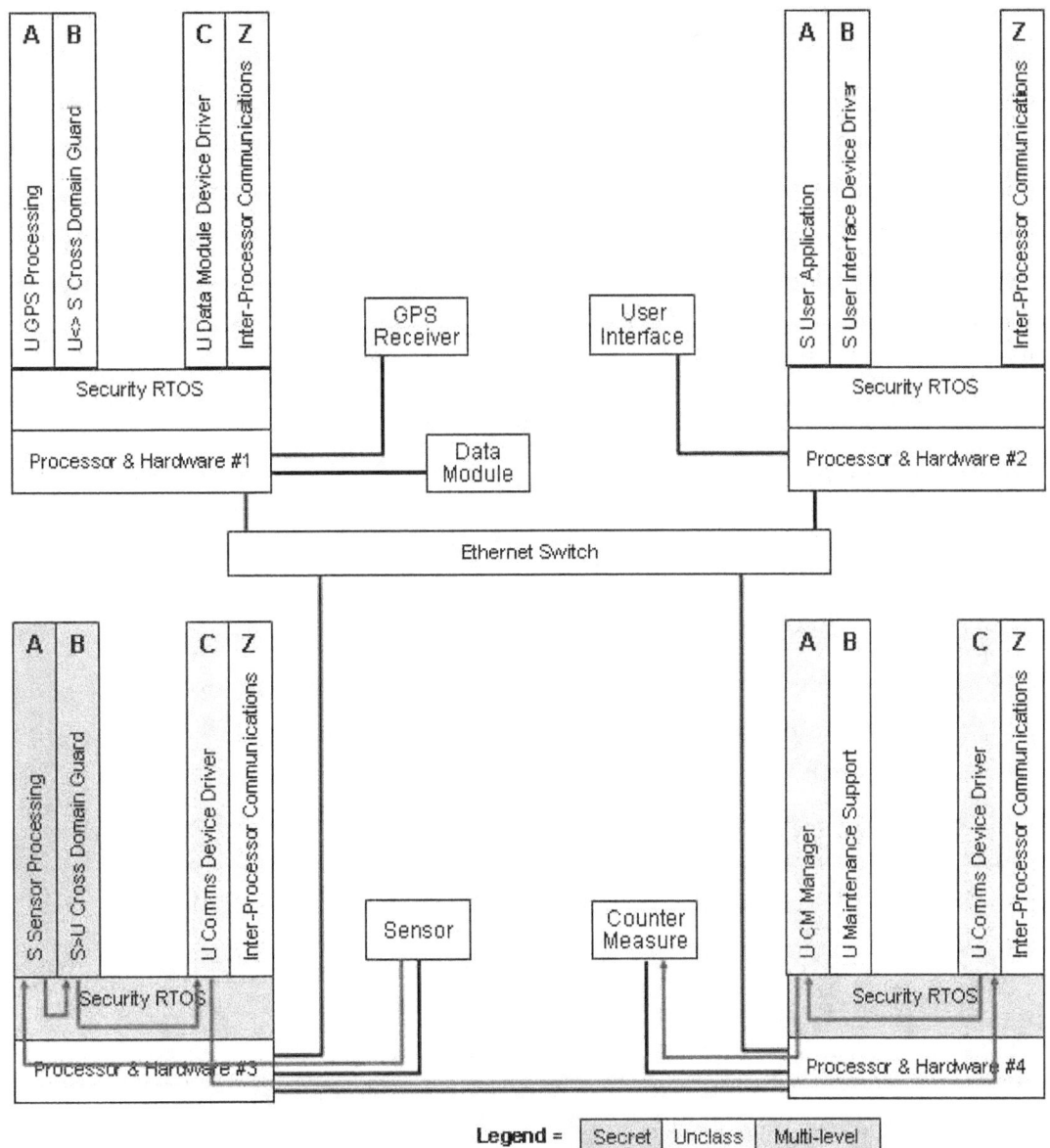

Figure 3: Scenario A Detect and Respond

- The command is passed from S Sensor Processing (3A)

- to S>U Cross Domain Guard (3B) where the data is examined to ensure no S data is present and is regraded as U and then

- the command is passed via the U Comms Device Drivers (3C and 4C) and the Dedicated Bus

- to U CM Manager (4A).

The Dedicated Bus is necessary to preserve the real time determinism required between Sensor and Countermeasure. After receiving the command, U CM Manager (4A) sends an instruction to Countermeasure that deploys a countermeasure to the imminent threat detected by the Sensor.

8.2.3.3 COUNTERMEASURE EXPENDED

The U CM Manager (4A) reports to U Maintenance Support (4B) that it has expended a countermeasure so the system knows it will need to be replaced at the next opportunity. U Maintenance Support (4B) passes the information to a Data Module that will be removed from the system after the mission and the data extracted and analyzed so that plans can be put in place to replenish the expended countermeasure.

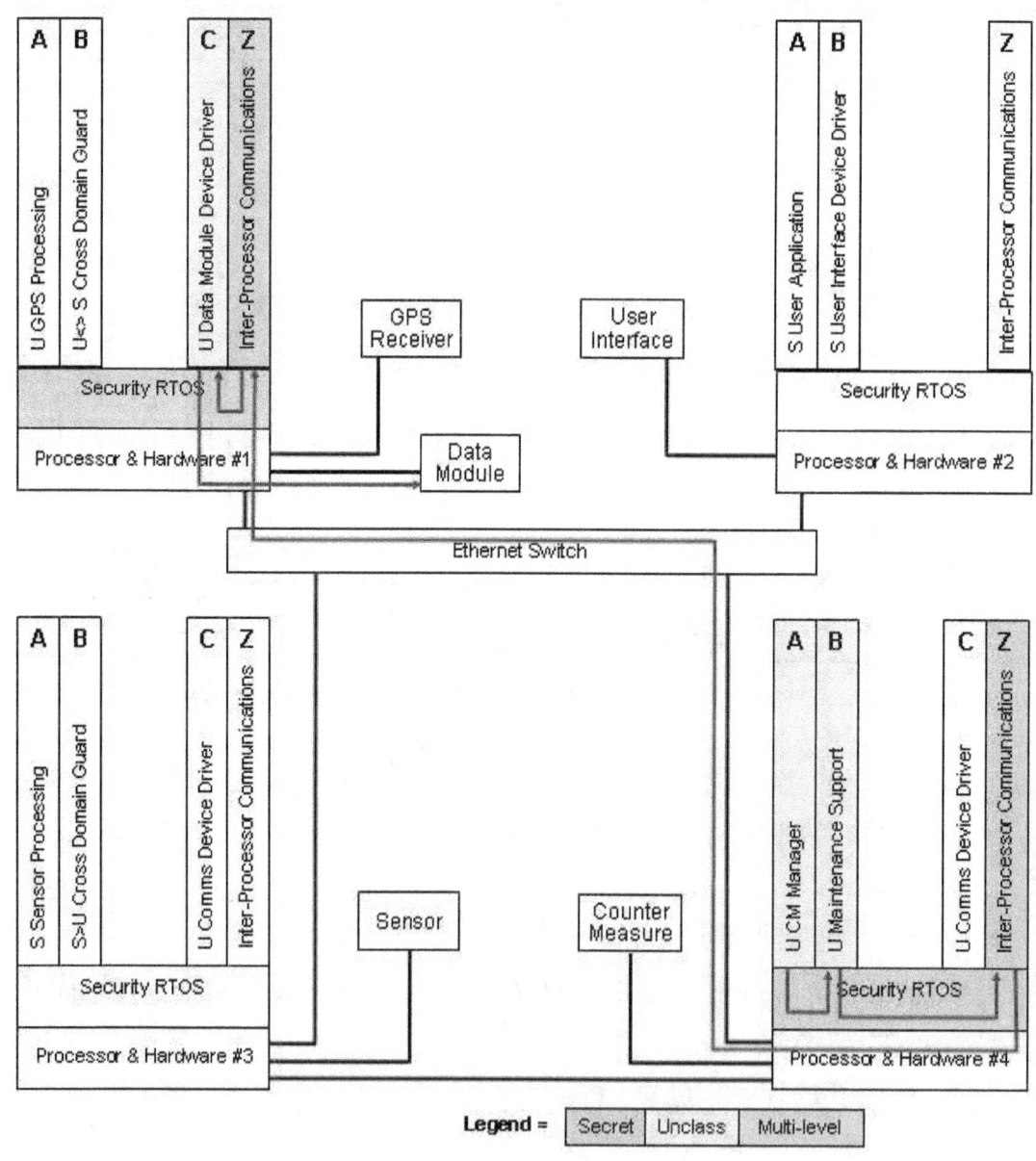

Figure 4: Scenario A Countermeasure Expended

- The expenditure of a Countermeasure is reported by the U CM Manager (4A) to

- U Maintenance Support (4B) which prepares a log entry and sends it via the Inter-Processor Communications (4Z and 1Z)

- to the U Data Module Device Driver (1C) which stores the data in the Data Module.

8.2.3.4 FUSED SITUATIONAL AWARENESS

The Sensor generates one of the inputs used to create situational awareness for the user. The Sensor outputs Secret data to S Sensor Processing (3A) where the data is processed/analyzed and then fed into the user's situational awareness (SA) (S User Application, 2A).

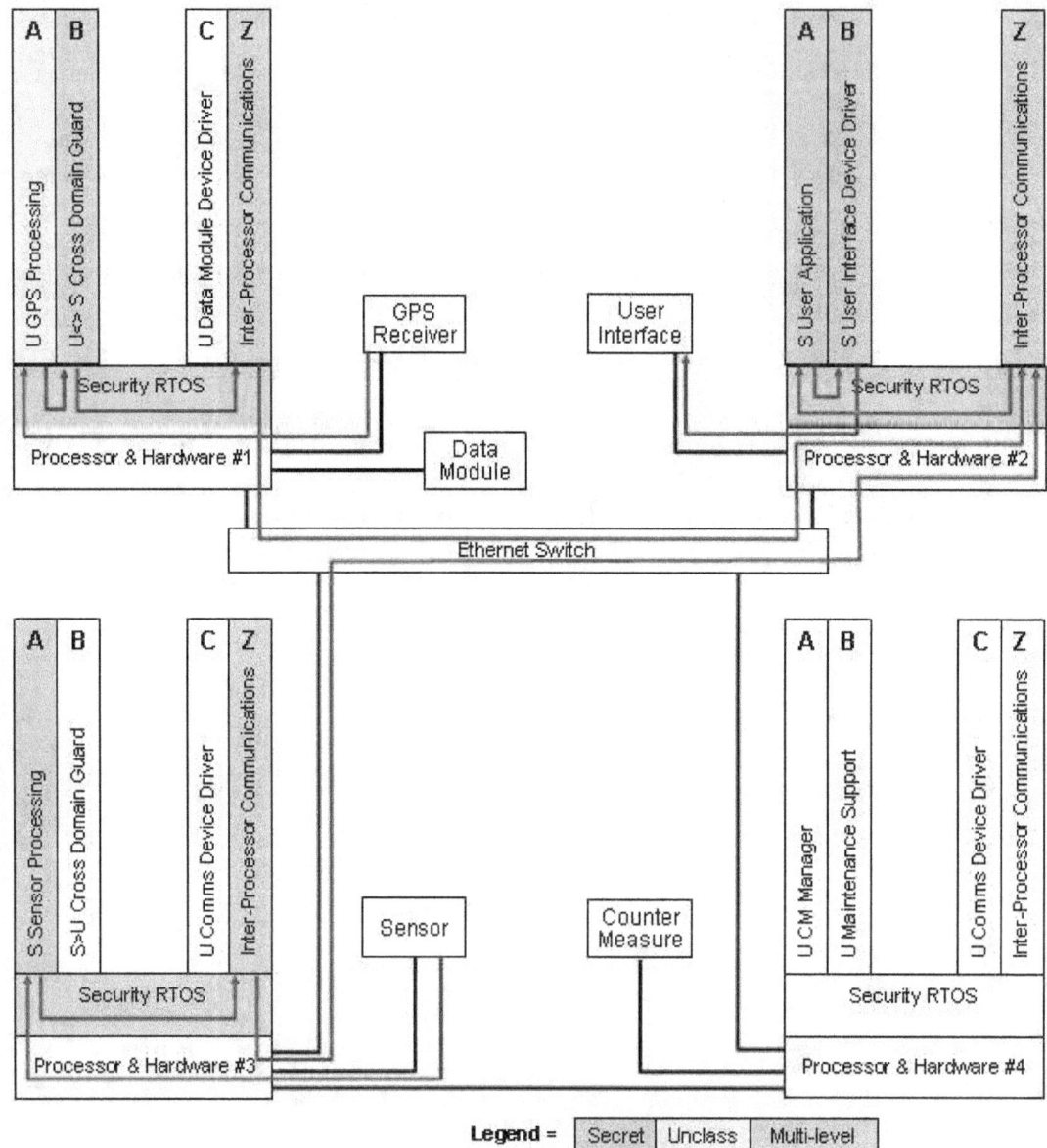

Figure 5: Scenario A Fused Situational Awareness

- Data moves from the Sensor to S Sensor Processing (3A) which provides its analysis of the data

- via the Inter-Processor Communications (3Z and 2Z)

- to S User Application (2A).

To maintain complete situational awareness (SA), S User Application (2A) receives information not only from S Sensor Processing (3A) as described previously but also receives location data from GPS.

- The location data from the GPS Receiver is passed

- to the U<>S Cross Domain Guard (1B) which regrades the data to S and sends it

- via the Inter-Processor Communication System (1Z and 2Z)

- to S User Application (2A).

The U<>S Cross Domain Guard (1D) ensures only harmless location data is passed to S User Application (2A). S User Application (2A) fuses all the data it has received and provides SA to the Secret User via the User Interface. S User Application (2A) interfaces with the User Interface via the User Interface Device Driver (2B).

8.2.3.5 REPORTING STATUS

S User Application (2A) provides basic status log information to the Data Module.

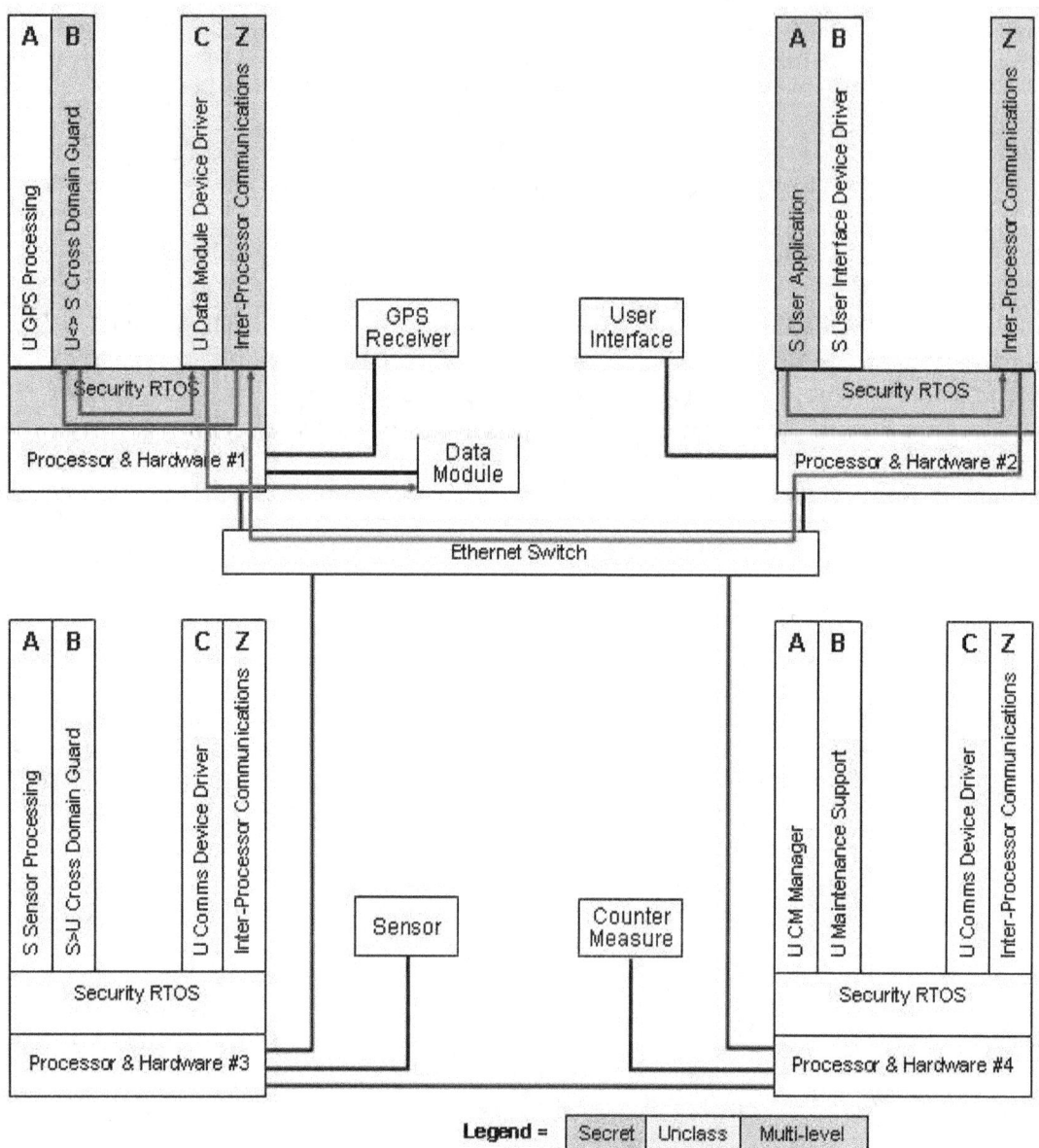

Figure 6: Scenario A Reporting Status

- S User Application (2A) sends basic reporting information

- via the Inter-Processor Communications (2Z and 1Z)

- to the U⟷S Cross Domain Guard (1B) and

- the U Data Module Device Driver (1C)

The U◇S Cross Domain Guard ensures that only strictly formatted status messages are sent from S User Application (2A) to the Data Module and that the messages contain no classified information. After the mission the Data Module is removed from the system and data is extracted and analyzed to perform post-mission analysis.

8.2.3.6 INFORMATION FLOW CONTROL POLICY

Several of the components in Figure 2 are responsible for enforcing security policies pertaining to information flow. The information flow control policy for each of those components is described below.

The Security RTOS (SRTOS) on Processor & Hardware #1 enforces an information flow control policy between the partitions running on Processor & Hardware #1 and between those partitions and the resources associated with Processor & Hardware #1 that are under the control of the SRTOS. The information flow control policy enforced by the SRTOS on Processor & Hardware #1 is as follows. All other information flows are not permitted by the SRTOS.

- U GPS Processing (1A) can send and receive information to/from the GPS Receiver

- U GPS Processing (1A) can send information to U◇S Cross Domain Guard (1B)

- U◇S Cross Domain Guard (1B) can send information to U Data Module Device Driver (1C)

- U◇S Cross Domain Guard (1B) can send and receive information to/from Inter-Processor Communications (1Z)

- U Data Module Device Driver (1C) can receive information from Inter-Processor Communications (1Z)

- U Data Module Device Driver (1C) can send information to the Data Module

- Inter-Processor Communications (1Z) can send and receive information to/from the Ethernet Switch

Inter-Processor Communications (1Z) enforces an information flow control policy between the partitions running on Processor & Hardware #1 and partitions running on any of the other three Processor & Hardware components. The information flow control policy enforced by Inter-Processor Communications (1Z) is as follows. All other information flows are not permitted by Inter-Processor Communications (1Z).

- U◇S Cross Domain Guard (1B) can send and receive information to/from S User Application (2A)

U⬦S Cross Domain Guard (1B) enforces an information flow control policy between partitions running in one security domain (classification level in the example) and partitions running in a different security domain (classification level in the example). The information flow control policy enforced by U⬦S Cross Domain Guard (1B) is as follows. All other information flows are not permitted U⬦S Cross Domain Guard (1B).

- U GPS Processing (1A) can send information to S User Application (2A)

- U Data Module Device Driver (1C) can receive information from S User Application (2A)

The Security RTOS (SRTOS) on Processor & Hardware #2 enforces an information flow control policy between the partitions running on Processor & Hardware #2 and between those partitions and the resources associated with Processor & Hardware #2 that are under the control of the SRTOS. The information flow control policy enforced by the SRTOS on Processor & Hardware #2 is as follows. All other information flows are not permitted by the SRTOS.

- S User Application (2A) can send and receive information to/from S User Interface Device Driver (2B)

- S User Application (2A) can receive information from Inter-Processor Communications (2Z)

- S User Interface Device Driver (2B) can send and receive information to/from the User Interface

- Inter-Processor Communications (2Z) can send and receive information to/from the Ethernet Switch

Inter-Processor Communications (2Z) enforces an information flow control policy between the partitions running on Processor & Hardware #2 and partitions running on any of the other three Processor & Hardware components. The information flow control policy enforced by Inter-Processor Communications (2Z) is as follows. All other information flows are not permitted by Inter-Processor Communications (2Z).

- S User Application (2A) can send and receive information to/from U⬦S Cross Domain Guard (1B)

- S User Application (2A) can receive information from S Sensor Processing (3A)

The Security RTOS (SRTOS) on Processor & Hardware #3 enforces an information flow control policy between the partitions running on Processor & Hardware #3 and between those partitions and the resources associated with Processor & Hardware #3 that are under the control of the SRTOS. The information flow control policy enforced by the SRTOS on Processor & Hardware #3 is as follows. All other information flows are not permitted by the SRTOS.

- S Sensor Processing (3A) can receive information from the Sensor

- S Sensor Processing (3A) can send information to S>U Cross Domain Guard (3B)

- S Sensor Processing (3A) can send information to Inter-Processor Communications (3Z)

- S>U Cross Domain Guard (3B) can send information to U Comms Device Driver (3C)

- U Comms Device Driver (3C) can send information to/via the Dedicated Bus

- Inter-Processor Communications (3Z) can send and receive information to/from the Ethernet Switch

Inter-Processor Communications (3Z) enforces an information flow control policy between the partitions running on Processor & Hardware #3 and partitions running on any of the other three Processor & Hardware components. The information flow control policy enforced by Inter-Processor Communications (3Z) is as follows. All other information flows are not permitted by Inter-Processor Communications (3Z).

- S Sensor Processing (3A) can send information to S User Application (2A)

- S>U Cross Domain Guard (3B) can send information to U CM Manager (4A)

S>U Cross Domain Guard (3B) enforces an information flow control policy between partitions running in one security domain (classification level in the example) and partitions running in a different security domain (classification level in the example). The information flow control policy enforced by S>U Cross Domain Guard (3B) is as follows. All other information flows are not permitted by S>U Cross Domain Guard (3B).

- S Sensor Processing (3A) can send information to U CM Manager (4A)

The Security RTOS (SRTOS) on Processor & Hardware #4 enforces an information flow control policy between the partitions running on Processor & Hardware #4 and between those partitions and the resources associated with Processor & Hardware #4 that are under the control of the SRTOS. The information flow control policy enforced by the SRTOS on Processor & Hardware #4 is as follows. All other information flows are not permitted by the SRTOS.

- U CM Manager (4A) can receive information from U Comms Device Driver (4C)

- U CM Manager (4A) can send and receive information to/from the Countermeasure

- U CM Manager (4A) can send information to U Maintenance Support (4B)

- U Maintenance Support (4B) can send information to Inter-Processor Communications (4Z)

- U Comms Device Driver (4C) can receive information from the Dedicated Bus

- Inter-Processor Communications (4Z) can send information to the Ethernet Switch

Inter-Processor Communications (4Z) enforces an information flow control policy between the partitions running on Processor & Hardware #4 and partitions running on any of the other three Processor & Hardware components. The information flow control policy enforced by Inter-Processor Communications (4Z) is as follows. All other information flows are not permitted by Inter-Processor Communications (4Z).

- U Maintenance Support (4B) can send information to U Data Module Device Driver (1C)

8.2.4 Component Robustness Level Guidance

The recommended assurance robustness levels for components within the Scenario A example system are shown in the table below and depicted in Figure 7: Scenario A Component Robustness Levels.

CATEGORY	ROBUSTNESS LEVEL	COMPONENTS
RTOS	Medium Robustness	SRTOS
Inter-Processor Communications	Medium Robustness	Inter-Processor Communications
Single-Level Applications	Basic Robustness or higher	S User Application S Sensor Processing U CM Manager U Maintenance Support U GPS Processing
Single-Level Commercial Off-The-Shelf (COTS) IA Applications	Basic Robustness or higher	This example does not include a component of this type, however it is feasible for such a component to exist in Scenario A.
Multi-Level Device Drivers	Medium Robustness	This example does not include a component of this type, however it is feasible for such a component to exist in Scenario A.

Single-Level Device Drivers	Basic Robustness or higher	U Comms Device Driver U Data Module Device Driver S User Interface Device Driver
Cross Domain Guards	Medium Robustness	U<>S Cross Domain Guard S>U Cross Domain Guard

Table 8: Scenario A Recommended Component Robustness Levels

The components for which Medium Robustness is recommended are all components where a failure within that component alone could result in the compromise of classified data (a breach in confidentiality). Basic Robustness would provide inadequate confidence that a breach in confidentiality would not occur. Medium Robustness, vice High Robustness, is appropriate for this scenario since the highest classification of the data is Secret, all direct users are cleared for all the data in the system, and all indirect users are relatively low risk to the system. The SRTOS provides partition isolation and information flow control between partitions on a processor, so its failure could result in Secret data being available to an unclassified process. The Inter-Processor Communication receives Secret and Unclassified data on one processor and delivers that data to Secret and Unclassified partitions on other processors, so its failure could result in Secret data being available to an unclassified process. The U<>S Cross Domain Guard (1B) passes data in both directions between Unclassified and Secret partitions so its failure could result in the compromise of classified data. The S>U Cross Domain Guard passes data from Secret to Unclassified partitions so its failure could result in compromise of classified data.

The components for which Basic Robustness is recommended are all components that are at a low risk of compromising data (breaching confidentiality) but do provide integrity and availability for the system. Basic Robustness is the minimum level recommended for these components. U GPS Processing (1A), U Data Module Device Driver (1C), S User Application (2A), S User Interface Driver (2B), S Sensor Processing (3A), U Comms Device Driver (3D and 4C), U CM Manager (4B) and U Maintenance Support (4C) perform important mission functions and could breach integrity or availability, but not confidentiality. In some cases, Medium Robustness or other increases beyond Basic Robustness may be appropriate for addressing privacy, availability, integrity and other concerns.

If a Protection Profile exists for any component at the appropriate robustness level compliance with that Protection Profile should be strongly considered as a requirement for that component.

The Ethernet Switch component is potentially a special case and is discussed in detail in Section 8.6.8.

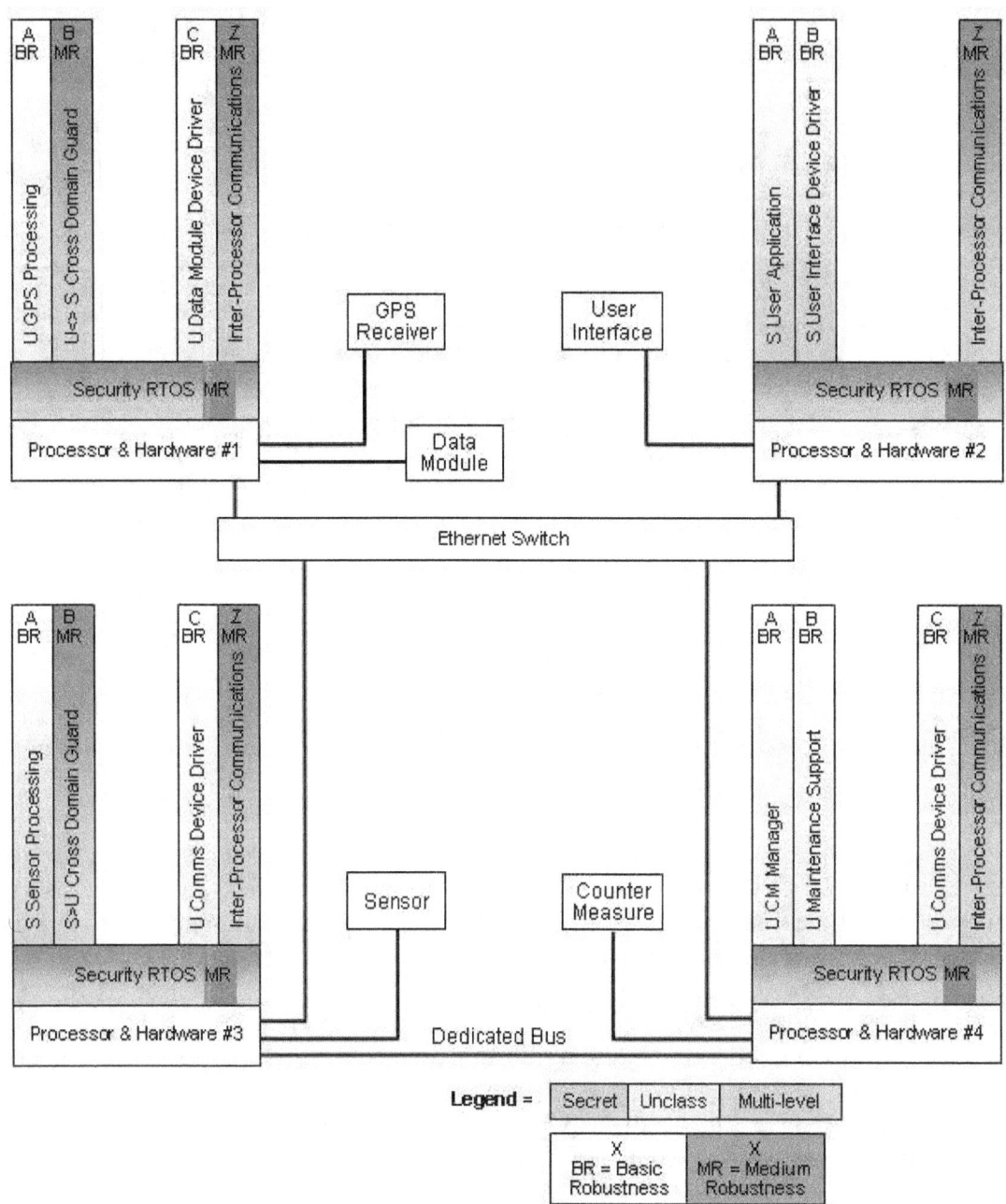

Figure 7: Scenario A Component Robustness Levels

8.2.5 Covert Channel Analysis Guidance

The purpose of the covert channel analysis is to identify and quantify covert channels and the associated residual risk. Covert channels could exist within a partition (for example a partition containing processes running at different classification levels), between partitions on a processor or between partitions on different processors.

All users in Scenario A are cleared to all of the data in the system. Because of this, a covert channel analysis is not recommended. There may be some covert channel analysis requirements on the components themselves (for example, a covert channel analysis on the cryptographic module to search for leakage of critical security parameters). However, a system level analysis is not necessary when all users are cleared for all data.

8.2.6 Privilege Mode Guidance

The minimal requirements for Scenario A for what should run in privilege mode are the Separation Kernel, any Architecture Support Package, and any Board Support Package. Since Medium Robustness is recommended for the SRTOS, additional code/applications could be run in privilege mode if needed. Special consideration should be given to any applications that might be of a time sensitive nature. Whenever feasible it is recommended that code/applications beyond those specified not be placed in privilege mode. Any code/application in privilege mode has full, unrestricted access to all memory, resources, devices, etc., and can circumvent the security policy. Therefore, it must be analyzed to gain confidence that it does not circumvent the security policy. Again, this discussion assumes a two mode world (user/kernel). However, if more modes are available to help further limit access, they should be encouraged. All code/applications, including runtime libraries and device drivers, running in privilege mode during operation should be Medium Robustness and are considered to be part of the SRTOS. Initialization and shutdown code or other code not executing during operation should also be Medium Robustness.

8.2.7 Protection Measures Guidance

Appropriate measures should be applied to ensure that unauthorized modifications to the system do not occur throughout its life cycle.

Procedures and security mechanisms are needed to ensure that any product with a role in enforcing the system's security policy has not been tampered with from its manufacturing/creation to its delivery (e.g. to the system integrator, application developer, or end user) and subsequent use. The integrity of the product must be protected during the initial delivery and any subsequent updates, and verified to ensure that the version used in the system matches the desired/intended manufacturer/vendor version.

Trusted delivery is used for the initial version distribution as well as for distribution of updates. Trusted delivery requires verification through procedures and/or tools that the version of the product used in the system and the desired/intended manufacturer/vendor version match. Electronic signature is a possible mechanism to use for trusted delivery of software. For hardware, shipment in containers that would show evidence of tampering is a possible mechanism. Incoming inspection could verify signatures on software and check for evidence of tampering with shipping containers.

There are several ways to mitigate the risk of integrating maliciously modified products. One such way is via a "blind buy." This is when the customer purchases a product using a pseudo-name to shield their identity from the vendor. There should also be consideration of the source of the product (offshore parts, etc.). Distribution and storage should also be taken into account.

After the system is delivered there is a risk that anyone with physical access to the system could modify and subvert the system. The unauthorized user must be prevented from maliciously altering the system. For example, an uncleared maintenance person could install a new product that had been maliciously modified. To mitigate this risk policy and procedures should control physical access to the system by anyone other than US persons with a clearance for all data that the system is approved to process. To detect inappropriate modification anti-tamper techniques such as tamper evident seals or other mechanisms are recommended. A person such as a maintainer may need to violate the anti-tamper in order to perform a needed function, and therefore must be cleared to the level of the system.

8.2.8   Guidance for Similar Cases

In some cases there may be only one classification level, but there is a need to isolate the data. An example would be a need to isolate security functions and data from other functions, such as separating audit functions from other functions. The guidance for Scenario A would apply to these cases as well.

In situations where Secret//Rel was used in Scenario A instead of U, the system would be processing Secret and Secret//Rel data. In this case, guidance for Scenario A would apply.

In this scenario the user is cleared for all the data in the system. If instead there had been an uncleared user then the guidance for Scenario A would still apply. Medium Robustness would still be adequate since the highest classification level of the data is Secret and the primary risk would still come from an insider, albeit now an authorized but uncleared user. If network connectivity were not limited then the change in risk would result in a recommendation to use the guidance for Scenario C.

8.3   IA GUIDANCE FOR SCENARIO B

8.3.1   Description of Scenario B

As described in the Environment Scenario section of this report, Scenario B reflects a system having the general characteristics summarized below:

- Physical Security: Security provided by the physical environment of the system is characterized as low risk. For example, the system is in a physically secure facility or it is protected as classified.

- Types of Users: The system holds users that are cleared up to Top Secret. Users are US users as well as non-US users.

- Security Domain Levels: The system processes Unclassified, Secret and Top Secret data on a single processor.

- Network Connectivity: The system is not connected to any significant external networks/systems, which would allow large numbers of remote people and processes any degree of access to the system. For example, the system may receive location data from a GPS receiver but it is not connected to the NIPRNet.

- Applications: The applications are limited. An example of a limited application is one that takes in data from a speedometer and adjusts a vehicle's throttle to maintain a constant speed.

- Protocols and Data Types: The system has limited protocols that are not in wide use and do not have known vulnerabilities published in open forums. For instance, the system may use a customized protocol for communications, designed to only work within that system. The data types implement fixed format messages, such as GPS messages.

8.3.2 Analysis of Scenario B

Primary areas of risk for Scenario B system described above include:

- Physical Security: The risk of unauthorized access that could jeopardize the security of the system is minimal because the system is in a physically secure facility and/or protected as classified Top Secret.

- Types of Users: There is an insider risk posed by the non-US user that is not cleared for all information processed by the system.

- Security Domain Levels: The system processes data from the Unclassified to Top Secret level. The value of the data is very high hence an adversary would be willing to apply significant resources towards compromising the data and unclassified processing within the system presents an exploitation opportunity for the adversary.

- Network Connectivity: There is a risk posed by the connections to external networks/systems. This risk will vary and requires examination of each connection to include the trust level of the user/process at the other end of the connection and the likelihood that information from that user/process could subvert the system. Since Scenario B has limited network connectivity the ability of an adversary to use this connectivity to access and attack the system is likewise limited and hence the risk is low.

- Applications, Protocols and Data Types: The limited applications and protocols and fixed data types make the system less likely to be exploited. This does not mean that one might achieve *security through obscurity* rather than from sound security engineering. Nor should one come to the conclusion that obscure software would permit security critical functions to be performed by low robustness software. Limited applications, data types, and protocols require an adversary to expend resources to obtain the necessary information and discover vulnerabilities. In the case of broad applications, data types, and protocols the information is readily known and vulnerabilities have already been discovered and published, and therefore represent no cost to the adversary

8.3.3 Example Scenario B System

An example system based on the characteristics of Scenario B is defined below and depicted in Figure 8 below.

The example system provides Top Secret cleared users (US and non-US) with fused situational awareness using data from within the system and from external input. The system includes a subsystem that can detect certain threats to the platform and respond with countermeasures.

Note that this is only an example of a system that would be consistent with the characteristics for Scenario B. The example system depicted here is only used to illustrate the IA guidance that would be appropriate for any system consistent with the characteristics for Scenario B.

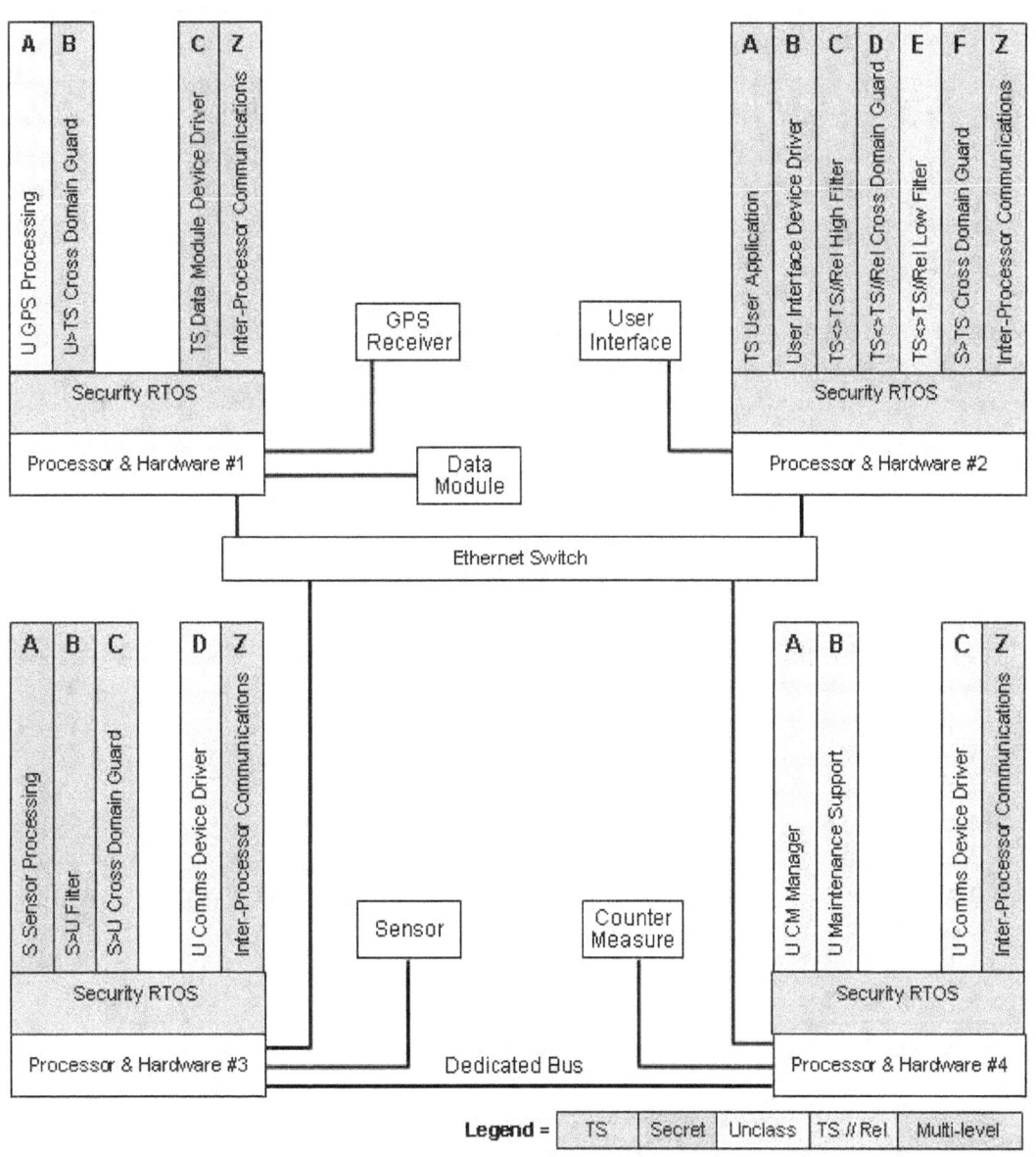

Figure 8: Scenario B

8.3.3.1 COMPONENT DESCRIPTIONS

The following paragraphs describe each of the components in the example system for Scenario B, as depicted in Figure 8. Partitions are represented by the vertical rectangles in the figure, such as "S Sensor Processing." A shorthand notation for referring to a particular partition is used in this document. The shorthand notation is the number for the "Processor & Hardware" hosting the partition and the letter shown in the figure for that partition. For example, U Maintenance Support is a partition on Processor & Hardware #4 and is labeled B, so its shorthand notation is 4B. If a partition involves data and processing at a single classification level then that level is included at the beginning of the name of that partition. For example, the "S" in S Sensor Processing (3A) indicates that this partition only processes Secret data. A "U" is used for unclassified data/processing, "TS" for Top Secret data/processing. An "S" or "TS" followed by "//Rel" indicates that the data/processing being performed is at some release level (releasable to another nation or set of nations). Partitions that support the movement of data between a partition at one classification level and a partition at a different classification level have two classification levels at the beginning of their name, as well as symbols to denote the direction in which the information flows. For example, the S>U Cross Domain Guard (3C) partition supports the movement of data between a Secret partition (S) and an Unclassified partition (U) with the information flowing from the Secret partition to the Unclassified partition (S>U). If information flows in both directions between the partitions "<>" is used, such as in TS<>TS//Rel Cross Domain Guard (2D).

Processor & Hardware represents the hardware components such as microprocessor, memory (volatile and non-volatile), interface devices, etc. This example system is based on four sets of hardware. This illustrates that most systems will have multiple processors and keeps the number of partitions on any one processor to a reasonable number for discussion. Note that the hardware could be the same for all four sets, but that would require that each set of hardware have all of the necessary interfaces. In particular: Processor & Hardware #1 requires a network interface (connection to the Ethernet Switch), a Data Module interface and a GPS Receiver interface; Processor & Hardware #2 requires one network interface and an interface to the User Interface device (perhaps a touch screen display); Processor & Hardware #3 requires one network interface, a Dedicated Bus interface and an interface to the Sensor; and Processor & Hardware #4 requires one network interface, a Dedicated Bus interface and an interface to the Countermeasure.

GPS Receiver represents a device connected to Processor & Hardware #1 that provides unclassified current location information to the system.

Data Module represents a device connected to Processor & Hardware #1 that provides data storage as a means for bringing Top Secret data into the system and taking Top Secret data away from the system. It represents a removable memory device.

User Interface represents a Top Secret (TS) device connected to Processor & Hardware #2 that provides a means for the user to interact with the system. It displays TS or TS//Rel situational awareness information to the user and it allows the user to enter information for composing situational awareness.

Ethernet Switch represents a device that interconnects the four Processor & Hardware components to allow the exchange of unclassified, Secret, Top Secret and TS//Rel data packets. The Ethernet switch just transfers the packets, and the only decisions it makes are related to the delivery of packets.

Sensor represents a device that monitors the surroundings of the system. It passes Secret information concerning anything it detects to the S Sensor Processing (3A) partition for analysis.

Countermeasure represents a device that deploys a countermeasure to protect the system from a threat detected by the Sensor. It is controlled by the U CM Manager (4A) partition.

Security RTOS represents the SRTOS that fulfills all the characteristics of an SRTOS as described in Section 6, Security RTOS Characteristics. It is all the software running in privilege mode on a processor. All other software exists in a partition. Each SRTOS enforces a policy that can control:

- what resources (memory, addresses, etc) are available to a partition (space partitioning)

- the amount of time or processor cycles provided to a partition (time partitioning)

- for a given partition, what other partitions on that processor the given partition can pass information to or receive information from (information flow control).

For example, partition 1A, U GPS Processing, would be allocated by the SRTOS on Processor & Hardware #1 a portion of the memory/address space available to the processor/SRTOS that would be sufficient for software running in the U GPS Processing partition. Partition 1A would also be allocated the address(es) necessary for accessing the GPS Receiver interface via Processor & Hardware #1. Partition 1A would be allocated a portion of the available processor cycles. Partition 1A would be allowed to receive information from the GPS Receiver and send information to partition 1B, U>TS Cross Domain Guard.

U GPS Processing (1A) represents a partition running at the unclassified level that controls the GPS Receiver device and receives position location data from the GPS Receiver. The current location of the system is used within other partitions to provide the user with situational awareness based on the user's current position and input from sensors, etc.

U>TS Cross Domain Guard (1B) represents a partition that performs a cross domain data transfer function. It takes in unclassified GPS data from the U GPS Processing (1A) partition, checks its format, etc, to determine the data is safe and then passes the data to the TS User Application (2A) partition so that the data can be used in providing situational awareness to the user. It also takes in unclassified Countermeasure usage data from the U Maintenance Support (4B) partition, checks its format, etc, to determine the data is safe and then passes the data to the TS Data Module Device Driver (1C) partition so that the data can stored in the Data Module.

TS Data Module Device Driver (1C) represents a partition running at the TS level that handles the interface to the Data Module device. It communicates with the TS Data Module via Processor & Hardware #1 and takes care of formatting data for storage on the Data Module. At a later time the Data Module is removed from the system and the reporting data is placed in another system for analysis.

Inter-Processor Communications (1Z, 2Z, 3Z, and 4Z) is described in Section 8.6.7. In summary, the four Inter-Processor Communications partitions connect via their respective Processor & Hardware to an Ethernet Switch that they share in common. These partitions support communication between partitions on different processors. Each of the four enforces its own security policy, which are subsets of the overall system security policy. For example, the Inter-Processor Communications (1Z) partition on Processor & Hardware #1 will allow partition TS User Application (2A) to communicate with partition TS Data Module Device Driver (1C) but would not allow TS User Application (2A) to communicate with partition U CM Manager (4A).

TS User Application (2A) represents a partition running at the TS level that takes in data from several sources, including the GPS Receiver, Sensor, Data Module and user, and fuses/composes a Top Secret situational awareness picture for the user. It also creates TS reports for storage on the Data Module to be extracted and analyzed at a later time.

User Interface Device Driver (2B) represents a partition running at the TS or TS//Rel level that handles the interface to the User Interface. It communicates with TS User Application (2A) or with TS<>TS//Rel Low Filter (2E) depending on whether the user is a US user with TS clearance or a non-US user with another nation's TS clearance. It communicates with the User Interface via Processor & Hardware #2.

TS<>TS//Rel High Filter (2C) represents a partition that performs a subset of the filtering necessary to ensure the flow of TS//Rel information up to the TS security domain will not harm the TS security domain and that only TS//Rel information flows from the TS security domain to the TS//Rel security domain. It works in conjunction with TS<>TS//Rel Cross Domain Guard (2D) and TS<>TS//Rel Low Filter (2E).

TS<>TS//Rel Cross Domain Guard (2D) represents a partition that performs a cross domain data transfer function. It takes in information from the TS security domain that has been filtered by TS<>TS//Rel High Filter (2C), verifies the filtering took place, and passes the TS//Rel information to the TS<>TS//Rel Low Filter (2E). Or it can take in information from the TS//Rel security domain that has been filtered by TS<>TS//Rel Low Filter (2E), verify the filtering took place, and pass the TS//Rel information to TS<>TS//Rel High Filter (2C).

TS<>TS//Rel Low Filter (2E) represents a partition that performs a subset of the filtering necessary to ensure the flow of TS//Rel information up to the TS security domain will not harm the TS security domain and that only TS//Rel information flows from the TS security domain to the TS//Rel security domain. It works in conjunction with TS<>TS//Rel High Filter (2C) and TS<>TS//Rel Cross Domain Guard (2D).

S>TS Cross Domain Guard (2F) represents a partition that performs a cross domain data transfer function. It takes in Secret data from S Sensor Processing (3A), checks its format, etc, to determine the data is safe and then passes the data to the TS User Application (2A) partition so that the data can be used in providing situational awareness to the user.

S Sensor Processing (3A) represents a partition running at the Secret level that takes in Secret data from the Sensor device and analyzes that data. If S Sensor Processing (3A) detects an immediate threat to the system (perhaps a missile coming towards a fighter plane) then it can initiate an action to respond with a Countermeasure (perhaps releasing chaff from the fighter plane to confuse the missile). S Sensor Processing (3A) also provides its Secret analysis of the data from the Sensor device to the partition TS User Application (3A) (via S>TS Cross Domain Guard (2F)) where that data is used to compose the Top Secret situational awareness for the user.

S>U Filter (3B) represents a partition that performs a data filtering function. It takes in a command to respond with a Countermeasure from the partition S Sensor Processing (3A), verifies the data is unclassified, etc, and then passes the command to the S>U Cross Domain Guard (3C). It works in conjunction with S>U Cross Domain Guard (3C).

S>U Cross Domain Guard (3C) represents a partition that performs a cross domain data transfer function. It takes in a command to respond with a Countermeasure from S>U Filter (3B), verifies the filtering was performed, and then passes the command to U CM Manager (4A).

U Comms Device Driver (3D and 4C) represents a partition running at the unclassified level that handles the interface to the Dedicated Bus. This partition exists separately on both Processor & Hardware #3 and Processor & Hardware #4.

51

Dedicated Bus represents a dedicated serial data bus that transfers information from Processor & Hardware #3 to Processor & Hardware #4. It is used to transfer the command to initiate a Countermeasure from Processor & Hardware #3 to Processor & Hardware #4. The Dedicated Bus interface on Processor & Hardware #3 can only be accessed by the U Comms Device Driver (3D) partition, a policy enforced by the SRTOS. The Dedicated Bus interface on Processor & Hardware #4 can only be accessed by the U Comms Device Driver (4C) partition, a policy enforced by the SRTOS.

U CM Manager (4A) represents a partition running at the unclassified level that controls the Countermeasure device and tracks usage of the Countermeasure. It reports usage of the Countermeasure to the U Maintenance Support (4B) partition.

U Maintenance Support (4B) represents a partition running at the unclassified level that receives information on the expenditure of Countermeasures and tracks Countermeasure usage. When replenishment of the Countermeasure is necessary the U Maintenance Support (4B) partition can store this unclassified fact in the TS Data Module (via U>TS Cross Domain Guard (1B)). After a mission when the data in the Data Module is analyzed the need to replenish the supply of Countermeasures within the system will be recognized.

8.3.3.2 DETECT AND RESPOND

If processing/analyzing of sensor data identifies an immediate threat then S Sensor Processing (3A) sends a command to initiate an appropriate countermeasure (CM) to the U CM Manager (4A). Since the command is originating in an S partition and going to a U partition it must pass through a Cross Domain Guard.

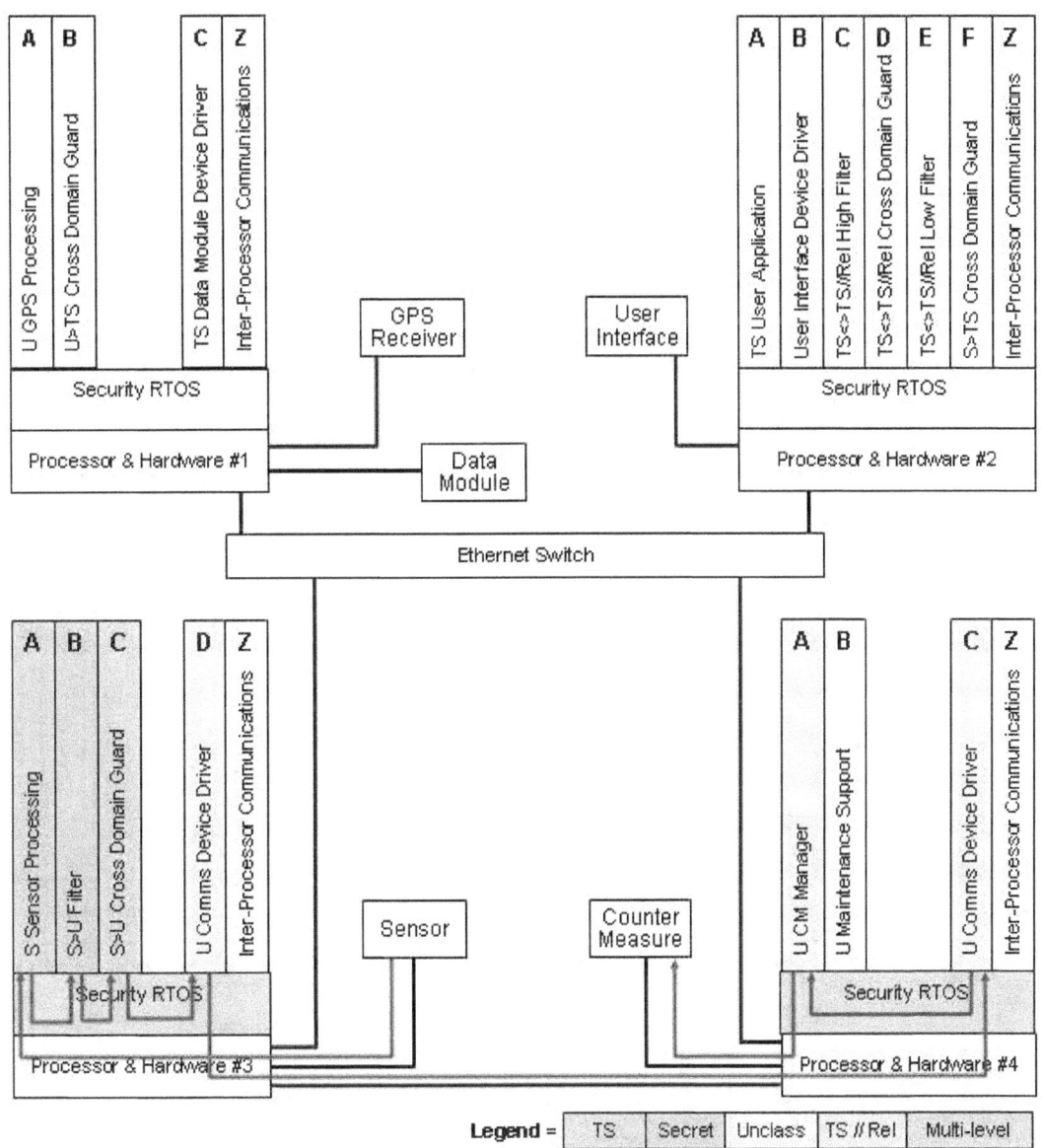

Figure 9: Scenario B Detect and Respond

- The command is passed from S Sensor Processing (3A)

- to S>U Filter (3B) where the data is examined to ensure no S data is present and then

- to S>U Cross Domain Guard (3C) where the data is checked and regraded as U and sent

- via the U Comms Device Drivers (3D and 4C) and a Dedicated Bus

- to U CM Manager (4A).

The Dedicated Bus is necessary to preserve the real time determinism required between Sensor and Countermeasure. After receiving the command, U CM Manager (4A) sends an instruction to Countermeasure that deploys a countermeasure to the imminent threat detected by the Sensor.

8.3.3.3 COUNTERMEASURE EXPENDED

The U CM Manager (4A) reports to U Maintenance Support (4B) that it has expended a countermeasure so the system knows it will need to be replaced at the next opportunity. U Maintenance Support (4B) passes the information to a Data Module that will be removed from the system after the mission and the data extracted and analyzed so that plans can be put in place to replenish the expended countermeasure.

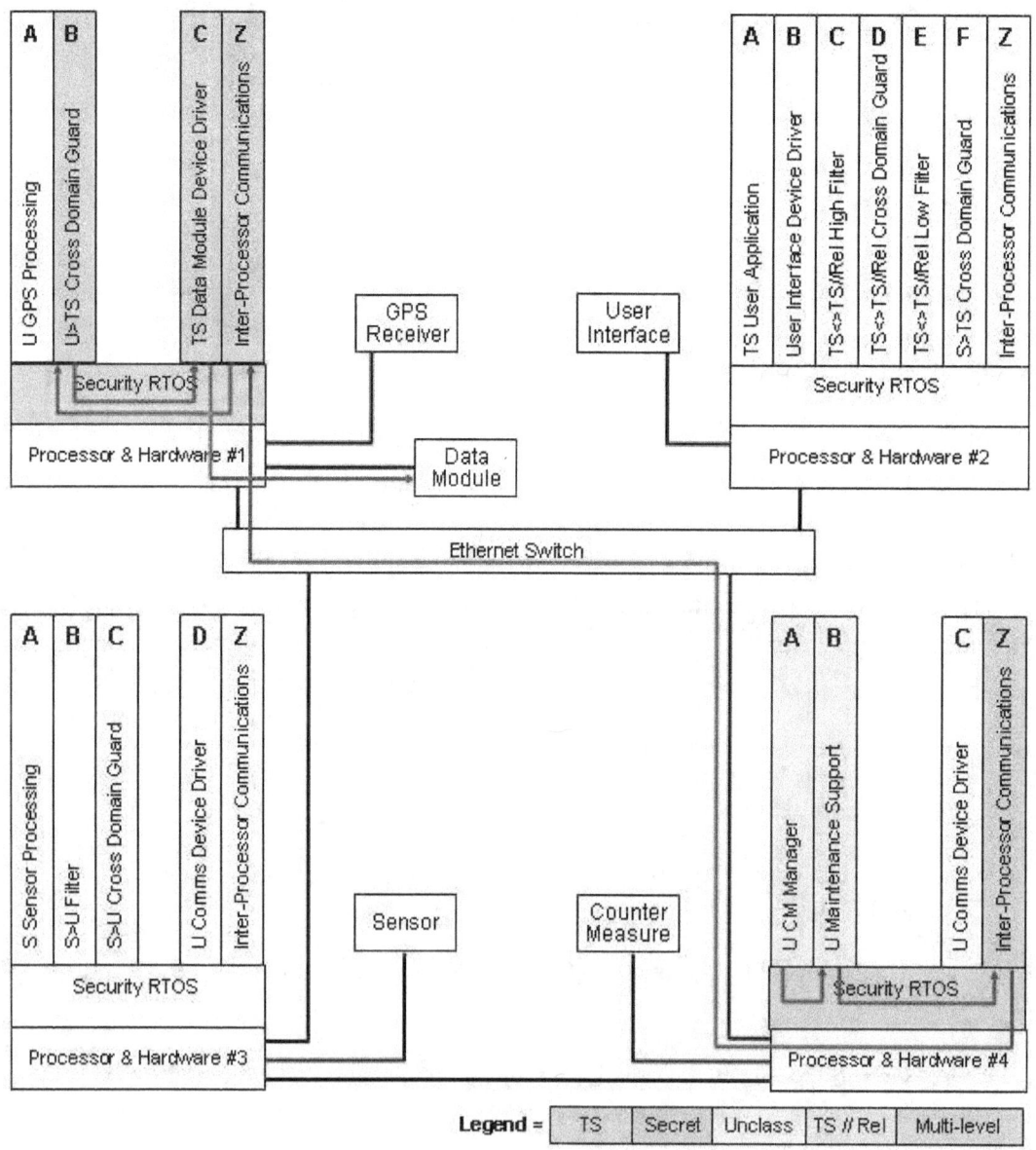

Figure 10: Scenario B Countermeasure Expended

- The expenditure of a Countermeasure is reported by the U CM Manager (4A) to

- U Maintenance Support (4B) which prepares a log entry and sends it via the Inter-Processor Communications (4Z and 1Z)

- to the U>TS Cross Domain Guard (1B) where it is checked to ensure it is properly formatted maintenance data and then regraded to TS and passed

- to the TS Data Module Device Driver (1C) which stores the data in the Data Module.

8.3.3.4 FUSED SITUATIONAL AWARENESS

The Sensor generates one of the inputs used to create situational awareness for the user. The Sensor outputs Secret data to S Sensor Processing (3A) where the data is processed/analyzed and then fed into the user's situational awareness (SA) (TS User Application, 2A). Since data is originating in a S partition and going to a TS partition it must pass through a cross domain guard.

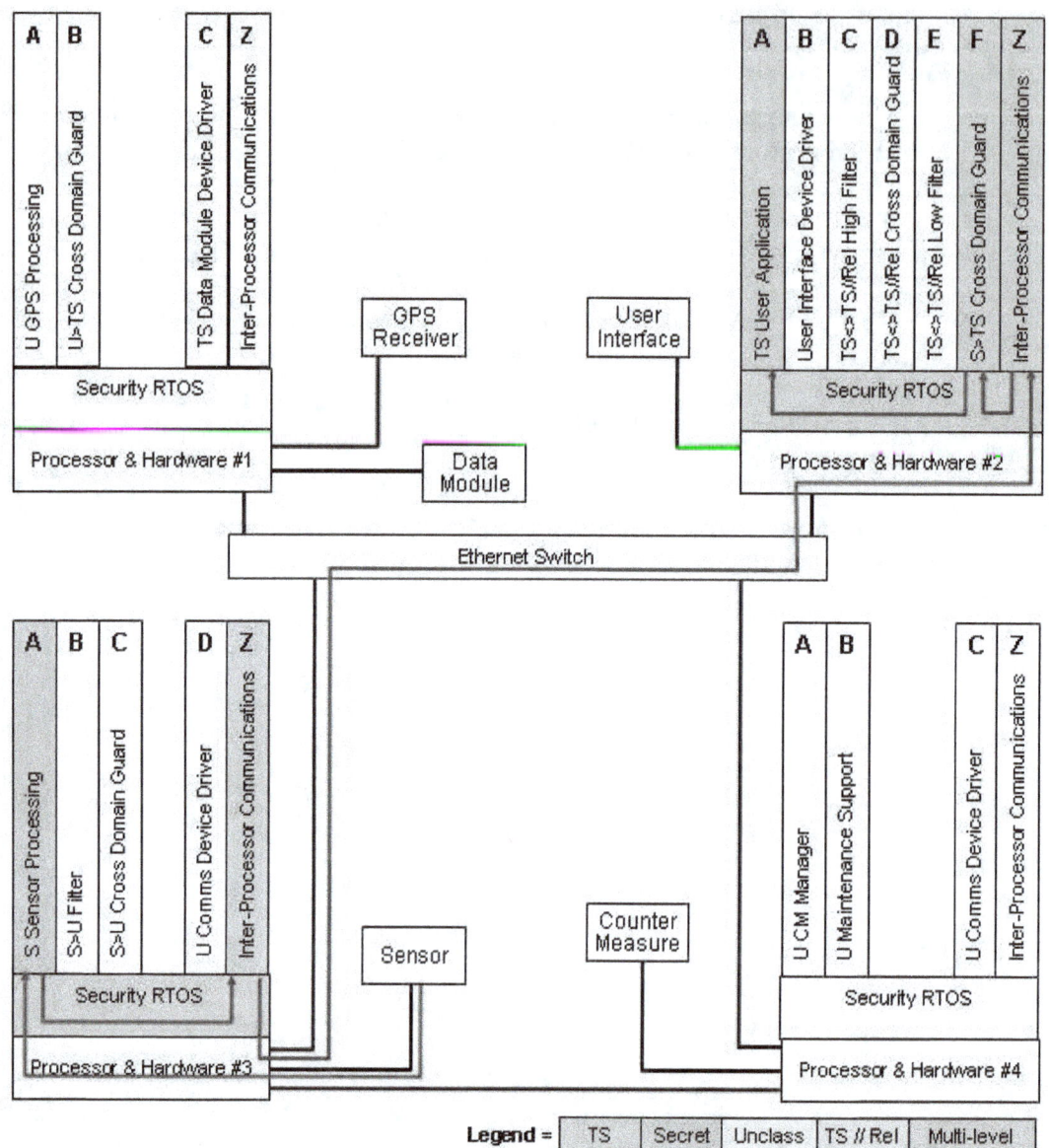

Figure 11: Scenario B Fused Situational Awareness

- Data moves from the Sensor to S Sensor Processing (3A) which provides its analysis of the data

- via Inter-Processor Communications (3Z and 2Z)

- to S>TS Cross Domain Guard (2F) where it is checked to ensure it is harmless sensor data and regraded TS and then sent

- to TS User Application (2A).

To maintain complete SA, TS User Application (2A) receives information not only from S Sensor Processing (3A) as described previously but also from the Data Module (information stored on Data Module and placed in the system at the beginning of the mission) and from the GPS Receiver.

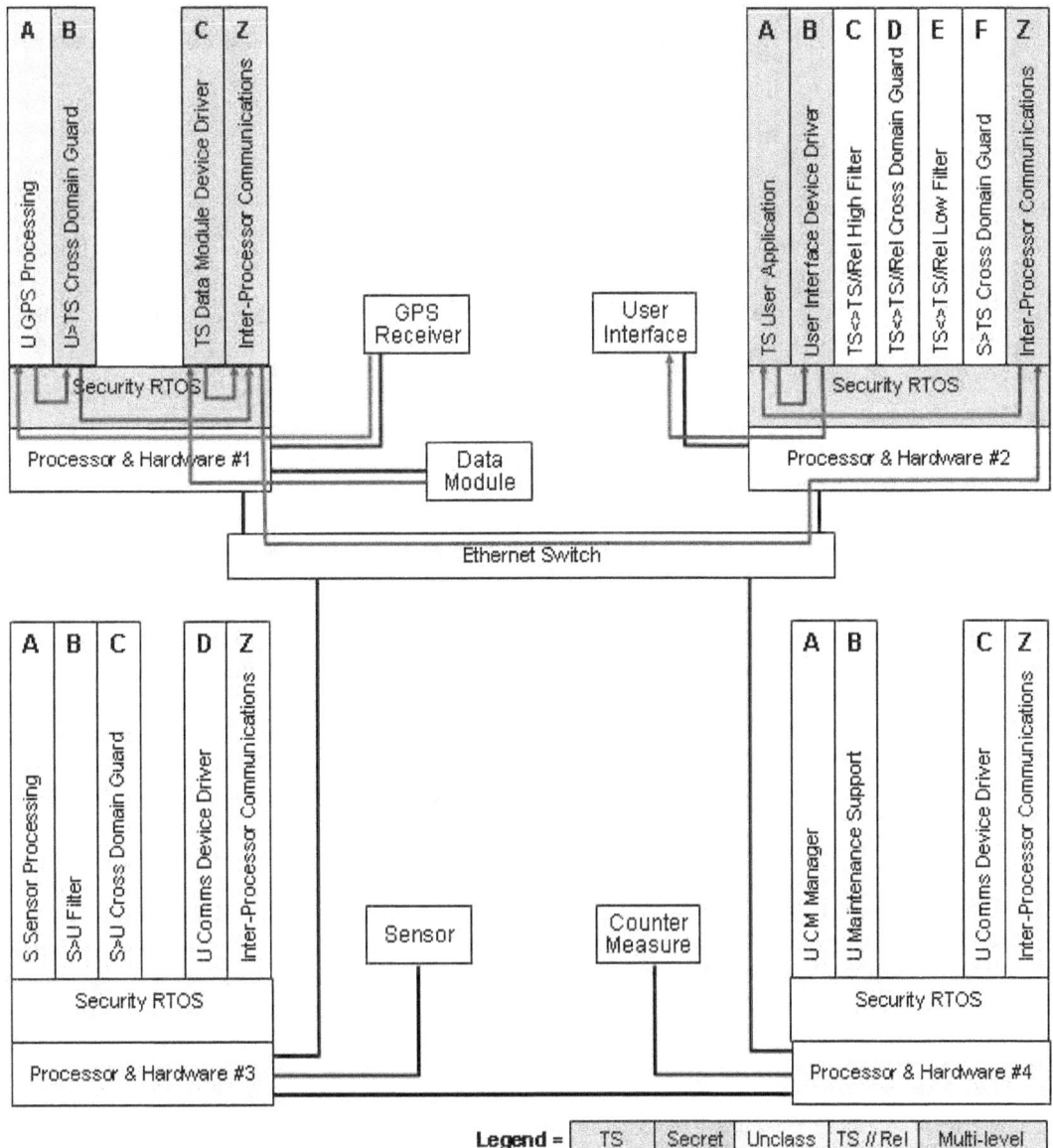

Figure 12: Scenario B Location Data Input to SA

- SA data from the Data Module is passed through the TS Data Module Device Driver (1C) and then

- via the Inter-Processor Communications (1Z and 2Z)

- to TS User Application (2A).

57

In addition to SA data from Sensor and Data Module, TS User Application (2A) also receives location data from the GPS Receiver.

- The location data from the GPS Receiver is passed to U GPS Processing (1A) and then

- to the U>TS Cross Domain Guard (1B) which regrades the data to TS and sends it

- via the Inter-Processor Communication System (1Z and 2Z)

- to TS User Application (2A)

The U>TS Cross Domain Guard (1B) ensures only harmless location data is passed to TS User Application (2A). TS User Application (2A) fuses all the data it has received and provides SA to the Top Secret US User via the User Interface. TS User Application (2A) interfaces with the User Interface via the User Interface Device Driver (2B).

8.3.3.5 FUSED SA AND THE NON-US TS USER

TS User Application (2A) also provides fused SA to the non-US TS user (TS//Rel), but the data must be sanitized before it is released to the TS//Rel user.

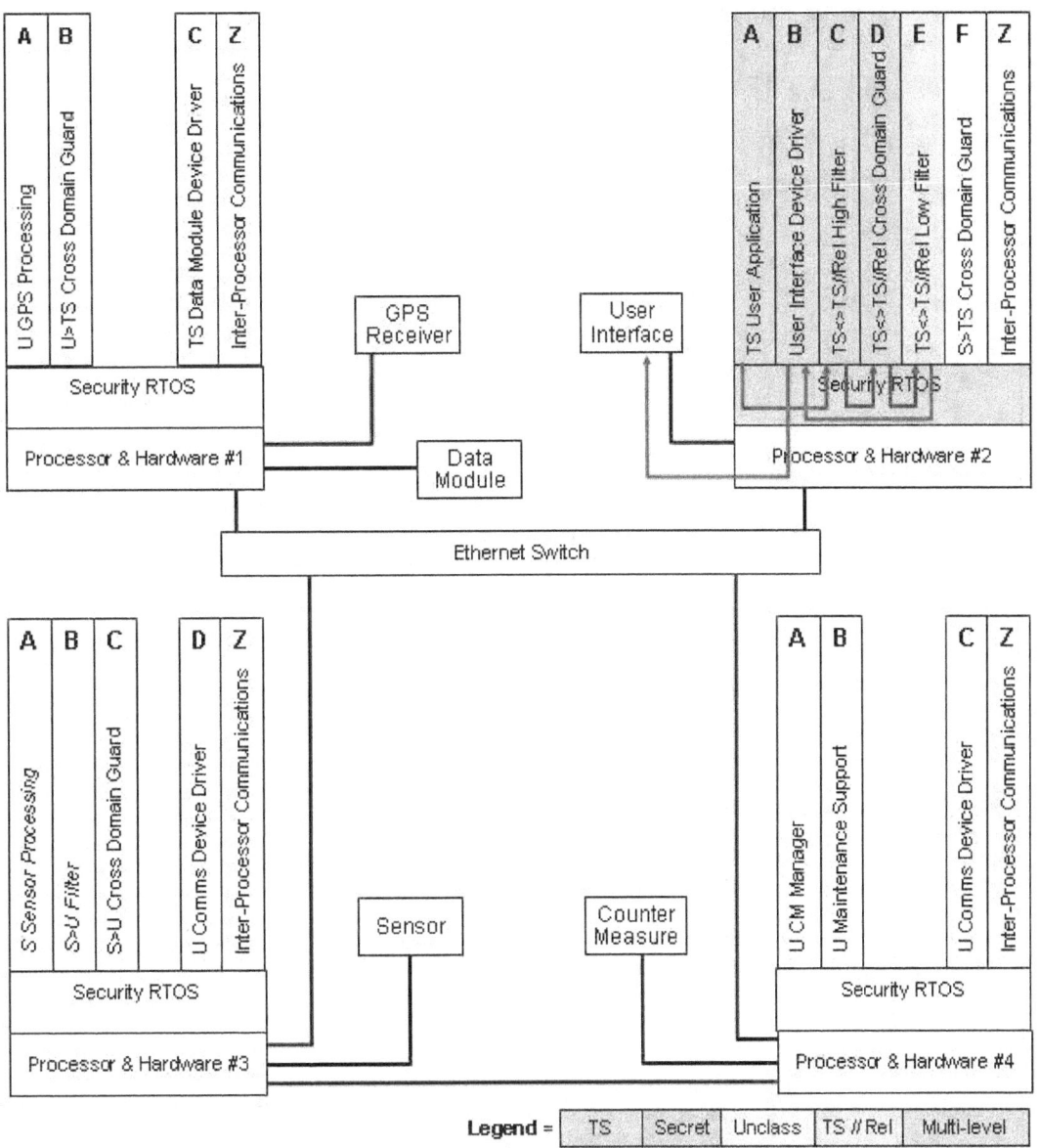

Figure 13: Scenario B Fused SA to the Non-US TS User

- TS User Application (2A) passes SA data

- via TS<>TS//Rel High Filter (2C)

- and TS<>TS//Rel Cross Domain Guard (2D)

- to the TS<>TS//Rel Low Filter (2E) and then

- to the User Interface Device Driver (2B) which interacts with the TS//Rel user via the User Interface.

TS<>TS//Rel High Filter (2C), TS<>TS//Rel Cross Domain Guard (2D), and TS<>TS//Rel Low Filter (2E) sanitize and regrade to TS//Rel the SA information so it is appropriate for release to the TS//Rel user.

Likewise, the TS//Rel user may enter data that must become part of the fused SA, so the data must be provided to the TS User Application (2A).

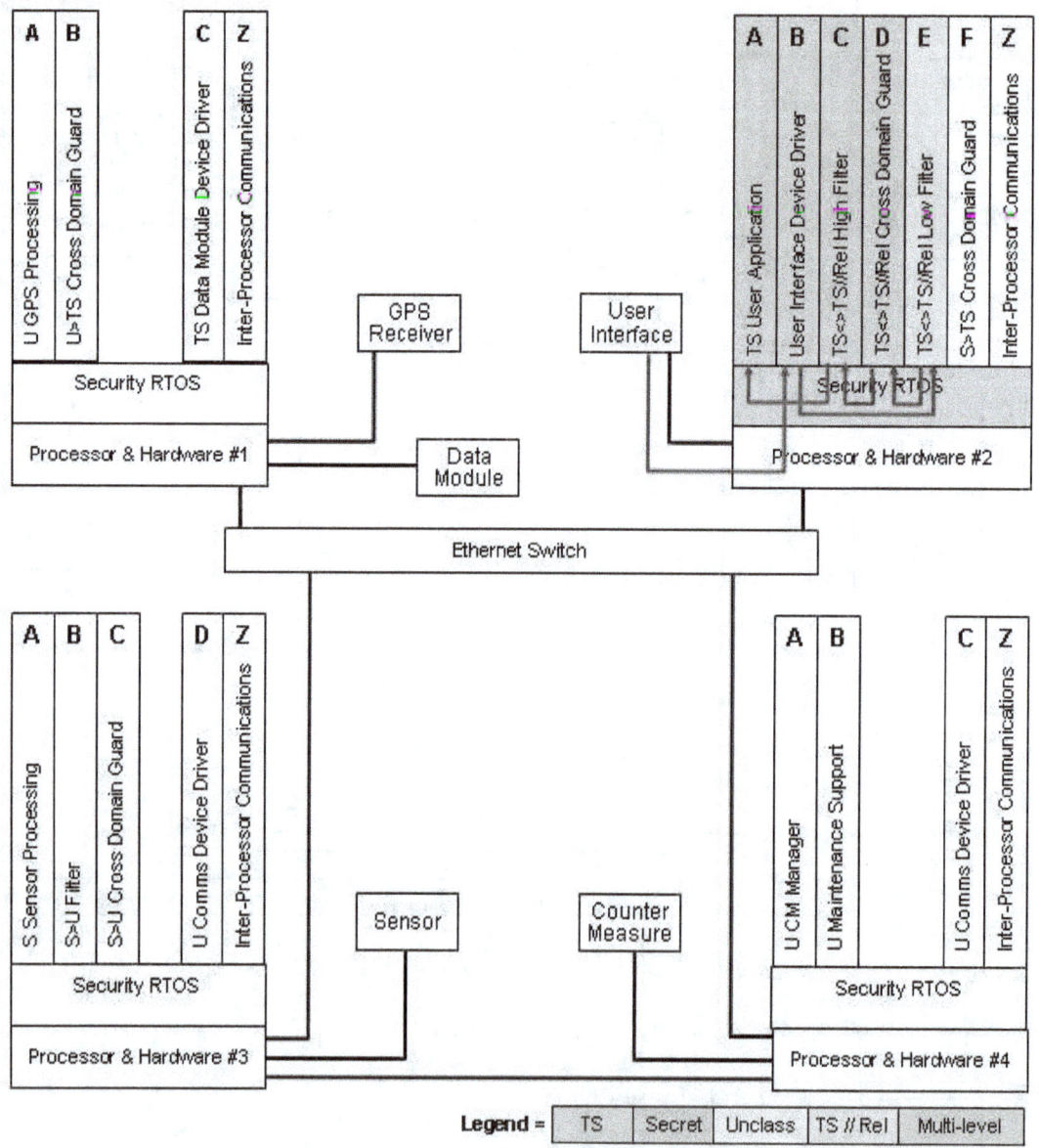

Figure 14: Scenario B SA Data from the Non-US TS User

- Data from the TS//Rel user is input via the User Interface and received by the User Interface Device Driver (2B) which sends it

- to the TS<>TS//Rel Low Filter (2E) and then

60

- to the TS<>TS//Rel Cross Domain Guard (2D) followed by

- the TS<>TS//Rel High Filter (2C) which passes the data

- to the TS User Application (2A).

TS<>TS//Rel Low Filter (2E), TS<>TS//Rel Cross Domain Guard (2D), and TS<>TS//Rel High Filter (2C) combine to check the data from the TS//Rel user to ensure it is appropriate and harmless and regrade it to TS.

8.3.3.6 REPORTING STATUS

TS User Application (2A) provides basic status log information to the Data Module.

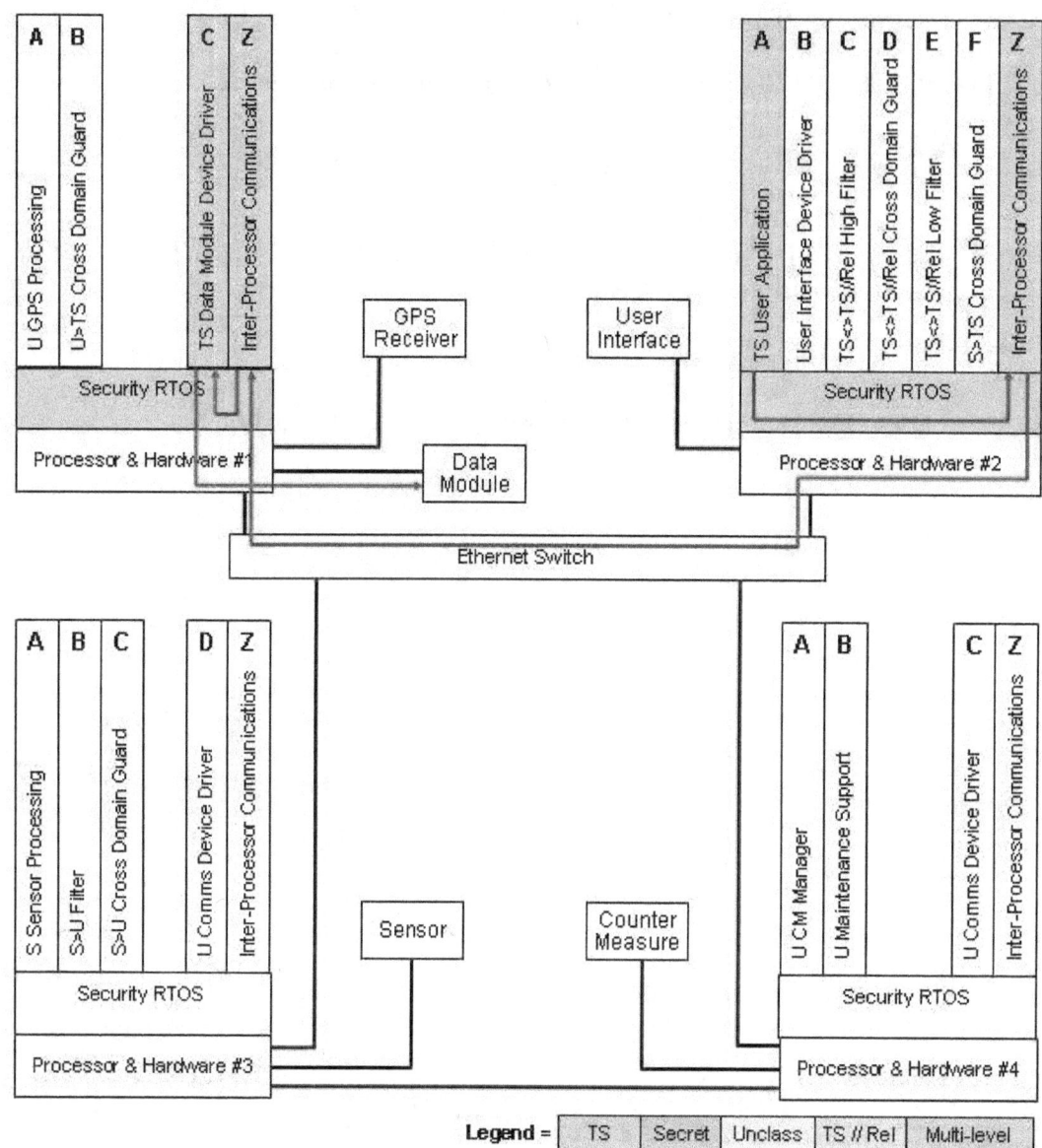

Figure 15: Scenario B Reporting Status

- TS User Application (2A) sends basic reporting information

- via the Inter-Processor Communications (2Z and 1Z)

- to the TS Data Module Device Driver (1C) which stores the data in the Data Module.

Note that the system that extracts data from the Data Module will be obtaining TS status log information and U maintenance data. That system must either handle all of the data as TS or be able to segregate the TS and U data appropriately.

8.3.3.7 INFORMATION FLOW CONTROL POLICY

Several of the components in Figure 8 are responsible for enforcing security policies pertaining to information flow. The information flow control policy for each of those components is described below.

The Security RTOS (SRTOS) on Processor & Hardware #1 enforces an information flow control policy between the partitions running on Processor & Hardware #1 and between those partitions and the resources associated with Processor & Hardware #1 that are under the control of the SRTOS. The information flow control policy enforced by the SRTOS on Processor & Hardware #1 is as follows. All other information flows are not permitted by the SRTOS.

- U GPS Processing (1A) can send and receive information to/from the GPS Receiver

- U GPS Processing (1A) can send information to U>TS Cross Domain Guard (1B)

- U>TS Cross Domain Guard (1B) can send information to TS Data Module Device Driver (1C)

- U>TS Cross Domain Guard (1B) can send and receive information to/from Inter-Processor Communications (1Z)

- TS Data Module Device Driver (1C) can send and receive information to/from Inter-Processor Communications (1Z)

- TS Data Module Device Driver (1C) can send and receive information to/from Data Module

- Inter-Processor Communications (1Z) can send and receive information to/from the Ethernet Switch

Inter-Processor Communications (1Z) enforces an information flow control policy between the partitions running on Processor & Hardware #1 and partitions running on any of the other three Processor & Hardware components. The information flow control policy enforced by Inter-Processor Communications (1Z) is as follows. All other information flows are not permitted by Inter-Processor Communications (1Z).

- U>TS Cross Domain Guard (1B) can send information to TS User Application (2A)

- U>TS Cross Domain Guard (1B) can receive information from U Maintenance Support (4B)

- TS Data Module Device Driver (1C) can send and receive information to/from TS User Application (2A)

U>TS Cross Domain Guard (1B) enforces an information flow control policy between partitions running in one security domain (classification level in the example) and partitions running in a different security domain (classification level in the example). The information flow control policy enforced by U>TS Cross Domain Guard (1B) is as follows. All other information flows are not permitted U>TS Cross Domain Guard (1B).

- U GPS Processing (1A) can send information to TS User Application (2A)

- U Maintenance Support (4B) can send information to TS Data Module Device Driver (1C)

The Security RTOS (SRTOS) on Processor & Hardware #2 enforces an information flow control policy between the partitions running on Processor & Hardware #2 and between those partitions and the resources associated with Processor & Hardware #2 that are under the control of the SRTOS. The information flow control policy enforced by the SRTOS on Processor & Hardware #2 is as follows. All other information flows are not permitted by the SRTOS.

- TS User Application (2A) can send and receive information to/from User Interface Device Driver (2B)

- TS User Application (2A) can send and receive information to/from TS<>TS//Rel High Filter (2C)

- TS User Application (2A) can receive information from S>TS Cross Domain Guard (2F)

- TS User Application (2A) can send and receive information to/from Inter-Processor Communications (2Z)

- User Interface Device Driver (2B) can send and receive information to/from the User Interface

- TS<>TS//Rel High Filter (2C) can send and receive information to/from TS<>TS//Rel Cross Domain Guard (2D)

- TS<>TS//Rel Cross Domain Guard (2D) can send and receive information to/from TS<>TS//Rel Low Filter (2E)

- TS<>TS//Rel Low Filter (2E) can send and receive information to/from User Interface Device Driver (2B)

- S>TS Cross Domain Guard (2F) can receive information from Inter-Processor Communications (2Z)

- Inter-Processor Communications (2Z) can send and receive information to/from the Ethernet Switch

Inter-Processor Communications (2Z) enforces an information flow control policy between the partitions running on Processor & Hardware #2 and partitions running on any of the other three Processor & Hardware components. The information flow control policy enforced by Inter-Processor Communications (2Z) is as follows. All other information flows are not permitted by Inter-Processor Communications (2Z).

- TS User Application (2A) can receive information from U>TS Cross Domain Guard (1B)

- TS User Application (2A) can send and receive information to/from TS Data Module Device Driver (1C)

- S>TS Cross Domain Guard (2F) can receive information from S Sensor Processing (3A)

S>TS Cross Domain Guard (2F) enforces an information flow control policy between partitions running in one security domain (classification level in the example) and partitions running in a different security domain (classification level in the example). The information flow control policy enforced by S>TS Cross Domain Guard (2F) is as follows. All other information flows are not permitted by S>TS Cross Domain Guard (2F).

- S Sensor Processing (3A) can send information to TS User Application (2A)

The Security RTOS (SRTOS) on Processor & Hardware #3 enforces an information flow control policy between the partitions running on Processor & Hardware #3 and between those partitions and the resources associated with Processor & Hardware #3 that are under the control of the SRTOS. The information flow control policy enforced by the SRTOS on Processor & Hardware #3 is as follows. All other information flows are not permitted by the SRTOS.

- S Sensor Processing (3A) can receive information from the Sensor

- S Sensor Processing (3A) can send information to S>U Filter (3B)

- S Sensor Processing (3A) can send information to Inter-Processor Communications (3Z)

- S>U Filter (3B) can send information to S>U Cross Domain Guard (3C)

- S>U Cross Domain Guard (3C) can send information to U Comms Device Driver (3D)

- U Comms Device Driver (3D) can send information to/via the Dedicated Bus

- Inter-Processor Communications (3Z) can send and receive information to/from the Ethernet Switch

Inter-Processor Communications (3Z) enforces an information flow control policy between the partitions running on Processor & Hardware #3 and partitions running on any of the other three Processor & Hardware components. The information flow control policy enforced by Inter-Processor Communications (3Z) is as follows. All other information flows are not permitted by Inter-Processor Communications (3Z).

- S Sensor Processing (3A) can send information to S>TS Cross Domain Guard (2F)

- S>U Cross Domain Guard (3C) can send information to U CM Manager (4A)

S>U Cross Domain Guard (3C) enforces an information flow control policy between partitions running in one security domain (classification level in the example) and partitions running in a different security domain (classification level in the example). The information flow control policy enforced by S>U Cross Domain Guard (3C) is as follows. All other information flows are not permitted by S>U Cross Domain Guard (3C).

- S Sensor Processing (3A) can send information to U CM Manager (4A)

The Security RTOS (SRTOS) on Processor & Hardware #4 enforces an information flow control policy between the partitions running on Processor & Hardware #4 and between those partitions and the resources associated with Processor & Hardware #4 that are under the control of the SRTOS. The information flow control policy enforced by the SRTOS on Processor & Hardware #4 is as follows. All other information flows are not permitted by the SRTOS.

- U CM Manager (4A) can receive information from U Comms Device Driver (4C)

- U CM Manager (4A) can send and receive information to/from the Countermeasure

- U CM Manager (4A) can send information to U Maintenance Support (4B)

- U Maintenance Support (4B) can send information to Inter-Processor Communications (4Z)

- U Comms Device Driver (4C) can receive information from the Dedicated Bus

- Inter-Processor Communications (4Z) can send information to the Ethernet Switch

Inter-Processor Communications (4Z) enforces an information flow control policy between the partitions running on Processor & Hardware #4 and partitions running on any of the other three Processor & Hardware components. The information flow control policy enforced by Inter-Processor Communications (4Z) is as follows. All other information flows are not permitted by Inter-Processor Communications (4Z).

- U Maintenance Support (4B) can send information to U>TS Cross Domain Guard (1B)

8.3.4 Component Robustness Level Guidance

The recommended assurance robustness levels for components within the Scenario B example system are shown in the table below and depicted in Figure 16.

Category	Robustness Level	Components
RTOS	High Robustness	SRTOS
Inter-Processor Communications	High Robustness	Inter-Processor Communications
Single-Level Applications	Basic Robustness or higher	TS User Application S Sensor Processing U CM Manager U Maintenance Support U GPS Processing
Single-Level COTS IA Applications	Medium Robustness	This example does not include a component of this type, however it is feasible for such a component to exist in Scenario B.
Multi-Level Device Drivers	High Robustness	User Interface Device Driver
Single-Level Device Drivers	Basic Robustness or higher	U Comms Device Driver TS Data Module Device Driver
Cross Domain Guards	High Robustness	U>TS Cross Domain Guard
Cross Domain Guards	Medium Robustness	S>TS Cross Domain Guard S>U Filter and S>U Cross Domain Guard TS<>TS//Rel High Filter and TS<>TS//Rel Cross Domain Guard and TS<>TS//Rel Low Filter

Table 9: Scenario B Recommended Component Robustness Levels

The components for which High Robustness is recommended are all components where a failure within that component alone could result in the compromise of classified data (a breach in confidentiality). High Robustness is appropriate for this scenario since the highest classification of the data is Top Secret and not all users are cleared for all the data in the system. Basic or Medium Robustness for these components would provide inadequate confidence that a breach in confidentiality would not occur (note the special circumstances described below). The SRTOS provides partition isolation and information flow control between partitions on a processor, so its failure could result in Top Secret data being available to an unclassified process. The Inter-Processor Communications receives Top Secret and Unclassified data on one processor and delivers that data to Top Secret and Unclassified partitions on other processors, so its failure could result in Top Secret data being available to an unclassified process. The User Interface Device Driver (2B) controls interactions with US Top Secret cleared users and non-US Top Secret cleared users via the User Interface and has access to both TS data from the TS User Application (2A) partition and TS//Rel data from the TS<>TS//Rel Low Filter (2E), so its failure could result in US Top Secret data being available to a non-US user. The U>TS Cross Domain Guard (1B) passes data from Unclassified to Top Secret partitions so its failure could result in the introduction of malicious code from an unclassified partition into a Top Secret partition.

To successfully be evaluated at a High Robustness level the size and complexity of a component must be reasonably small. At present, expectations are that an RTOS, Inter-Processor Communication, and some cross domain guards (such as the one in partition 1B) can achieve High Robustness. However, some cross domain guards will likely not be able to achieve High Robustness. In cases such as this the guidance below applies.

The components for which Medium Robustness is recommended are critical components of a distributed cross domain guard and a cross domain guard separating S from TS. If the requirement is for the one-way transfer of data from Secret to Unclassified, a Medium Robustness cross domain guard could be used if a complementary Medium Robustness security filtering application is implemented on the Secret side of the cross domain guard in a separate partition. This is depicted by the S>U Filter (3B) and S>U Cross Domain Guard (3C) partitions in Scenario B. Since a one-way transfer of data basically limits an adversary to attempting to install malicious code (via a low-to-high data transfer), or to obtaining classified data only when an error is made on the high side (inadvertent disclosure via a high-to-low data transfer), it may be sufficient to implement appropriate filtering and guarding functions at Medium Robustness in a complementary manner. Note that the filter component should always be at the highest security level irrespective of whether the data is flowing from the higher security level to a lower level or lower security level to higher level.

If the requirement is for the bidirectional transfer of data between TS and TS//Rel a Medium Robustness cross domain guard could be used if complementary Medium Robustness security filtering applications are implemented on the TS side of the cross domain guard and on the TS//Rel side of the cross domain guard in separate partitions. This is depicted by the TS<>TS//Rel High Filter (2C), TS<>TS//Rel Cross Domain Guard (2D), and the TS<>TS//Rel Low Filter (2E) partitions in Scenario B.

Since a bidirectional transfer of data basically permits an adversary to attempt to install malicious code (via a low-to-high data transfer) and then obtain unauthorized data (via a high-to-low data transfer) a thorough and complementary implementation of security mechanisms across all three partitions at Medium Robustness may be sufficient.

The layering of independent but complementary security functions/checks in multiple partitions can often be used to reduce the robustness level of any one component. An analogy in cryptography would be triple Data Encryption Standard (DES). Triple DES uses three independent and complementary instantiations of DES. While an adversary may have the resources to determine the underlying data if it is protected by DES, layering in the manner used for triple DES dramatically increases the adversary's cost and so long as that cost is then higher than the adversary is willing or able to pay then adequate protection is achieved. In this example system a similar approach is described for implementing a cross domain solution comprised of multiple Medium Robustness components, hence causing the adversary's cost to increase since each component would need to be subverted. A similar approach could be used for the Inter-Processor Communications. If the Inter-Processor Communications (IPC) partition was divided into two independent security functions/partitions, one checking data received and one checking data sent, then an adversary would need to subvert/defeat both the "transmit" IPC and the "receive" IPC in order to pass unauthorized data from one processor to another. If the transmit and receive components did not share a common flaw then the adversary must expend resources to find two complementary flaws. It is possible that the transmit and receive components could be Medium Robustness and provide adequate protection. When using this layering approach it is important that the partitions be independent (the same flaw is unlikely to exist in both) and complementary (a security breach requires breaching all of the layers). It would likely be impractical to apply this approach to the SRTOS.

In the situation where the Cross Domain Guard is separating S from TS, such as S>TS Cross Domain Guard (2F), Medium Robustness is recommended. High Robustness is not necessarily needed because the guard is not separating the full range of the system, unclassified to Top Secret, and the guard is only providing for the one-way transfer of data from S to TS.

Although TS and TS//Rel may appear to be at the same security level they should be considered as different security levels since not all parties hold the same clearance (US users hold a US Top Secret clearance, Nation X users hold a Nation X Top Secret clearance). This is different than compartmented/SAR/Special Access Program (SAP) data protection where all users hold the same US clearance but some have not been granted formal access approval to the compartmented/SAR/SAP data.

In cases where the cross domain guard is interconnecting TS and TS//Rel environments (such as TS<>TS//Rel Cross Domain Guard (2D)) the threat represented by the coalition or ally can be used as a factor in determining the capabilities and assurance of the cross domain guard and filters. If the TS//Rel environment is highly trusted then there is less risk that it will attempt to subvert the TS environment and appropriate trade-offs can be made on data types permitted to traverse the cross domain guard and the assurance level of the cross domain guard. Even for most trusted allies an assurance level of at least Medium Robustness is recommended. This guidance would also apply to User Interface Device Driver (2B) that is being relied on to protect TS from the TS//Rel user.

The components for which Basic Robustness is recommended are all components that are at a low risk of compromising data (breaching confidentiality) but do provide integrity and availability for the system. Basic Robustness is the minimum level recommended for these components. S User Application (2A), U User Browser Application (2F), S Sensor Processing (3A) and U Comms Device Driver (3D and 4C) perform important mission functions and could breach integrity or availability but not confidentiality. In some cases, Medium Robustness or other increases beyond Basic Robustness may be appropriate for addressing privacy, availability, integrity and other concerns.

If a Protection Profile exists for any component at the appropriate robustness level compliance with that Protection Profile should be strongly considered as a requirement for that component.

The Ethernet Switch component is potentially a special case and is discussed in detail in Section 8.6.8.

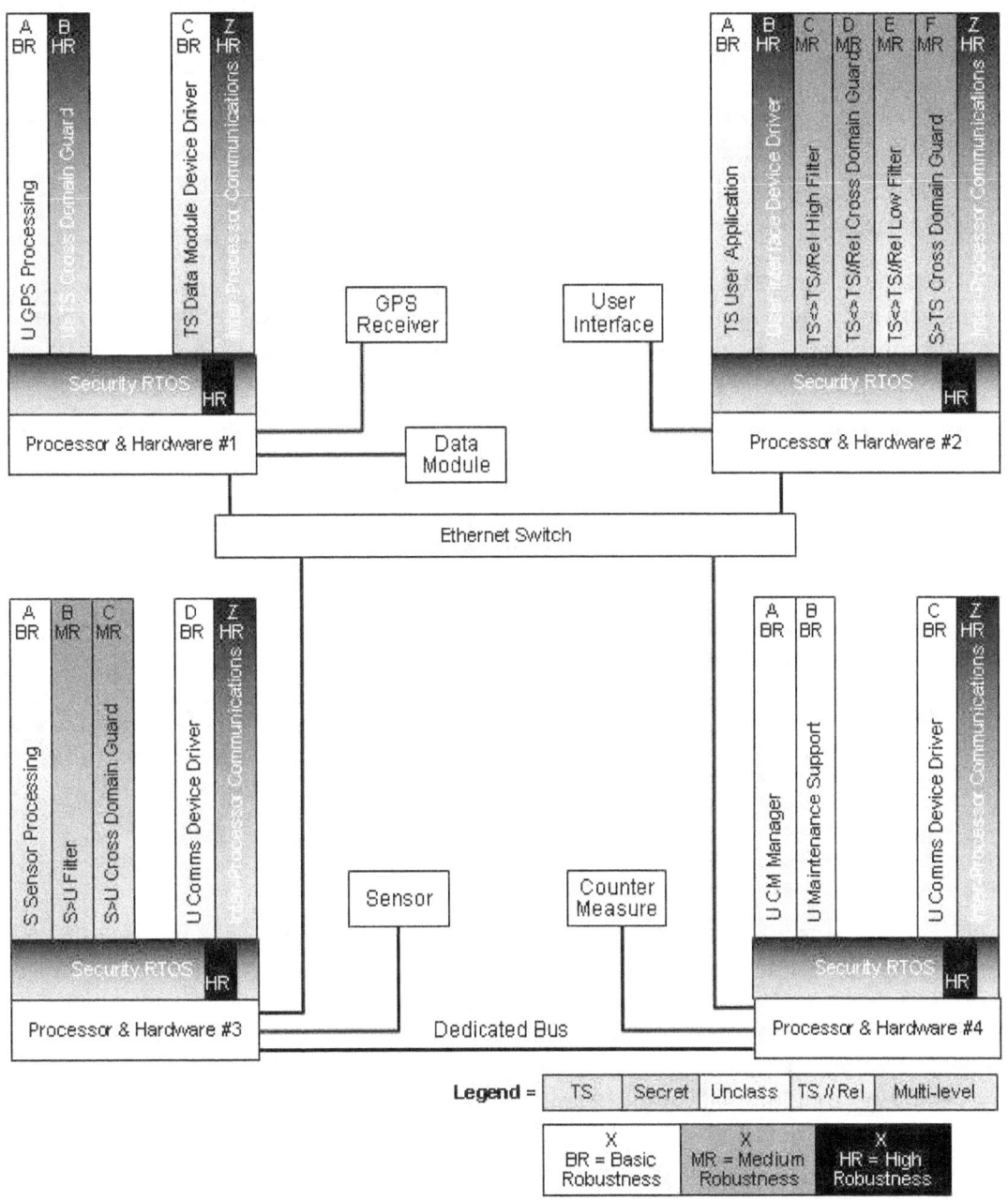

Figure 16: Scenario B Component Robustness Levels

8.3.5   Covert Channel Analysis Guidance

The purpose of the covert channel analysis is to identify and quantify covert channels and the associated residual risk. Covert channels could exist within a partition (for example a partition containing processes running at different classification levels), between partitions on a processor or between partitions on different processors.

A systematic covert channel analysis is recommended for the Scenario B system. This is recommended because Top Secret data resides on the system, and some users are not cleared for all of the data, including users with non-US clearances such as in the TS//Rel cases. The covert channel analysis should pay particular attention to the areas where cryptography is being used in the system, as well as to the data that can affect the cryptography in the system. Additionally, there may be additional covert channel analysis requirements levied on the components that make up the system.

Some covert channels cannot be eliminated due to real time constraints and the need for efficient access to shared resources. The certifier and accreditor of the system must ultimately decide on what level of risk is acceptable with regard to covert channels.

8.3.6 Privilege Mode Guidance

The minimal requirements for Scenario B for what should run in privilege mode are the Separation Kernel, any Architecture Support Package, and any Board Support Package. Since High Robustness is recommended for the SRTOS, additional code/applications should not be run in privilege mode. Any code/application in privilege mode has full, unrestricted access to all memory, resources, devices, etc, and can circumvent the security policy.

All code/applications, including runtime libraries and device drivers, running in privilege mode during operation should be High Robustness and are considered to be part of the SRTOS. Initialization and shutdown code or other code not executing during operation should also be High Robustness.

8.3.7 Protection Measures Guidance

Appropriate measures should be applied to ensure that unauthorized modifications to the system do not occur throughout its life cycle.

Procedures and security mechanisms are needed to ensure that any product with a role in enforcing the system's security policy has not been tampered with from its manufacturing/creation to its delivery (e.g. to the system integrator, application developer, or end user) and subsequent use. The integrity of the product must be protected during the initial delivery and any subsequent updates, and verified to ensure that the version used in the system matches the desired/intended manufacturer/vendor version.

Trusted delivery is used for the initial version distribution as well as for distribution of updates. Trusted delivery requires verification through procedures and/or tools that the version of the product used in the system and the desired/intended manufacturer/vendor version match. Electronic signature is a possible mechanism to use for trusted delivery of software. For hardware, shipment in containers that would show evidence of tampering is a possible mechanism. Incoming inspection could verify signatures on software and check for evidence of tampering with shipping containers.

There are several ways to mitigate the risk of integrating maliciously modified products. One such way is via a "blind buy." This is when the customer purchases a product using a pseudo-name to shield their identity from the vendor. There should also be consideration of the source of the product (offshore parts, etc.). Distribution and storage should also be taken into account.

After the system is delivered there is a risk that anyone with physical access to the system could modify and subvert the system. The unauthorized user must be prevented from maliciously altering the system. For example, an uncleared maintenance person could install a new product that had been maliciously modified. To mitigate this risk policy and procedures should control physical access to the system by anyone other than US persons with a clearance for all data that the system is approved to process. To detect inappropriate modification anti-tamper techniques such as tamper evident seals or other mechanisms are recommended. A person such as a maintainer may need to violate the anti-tamper in order to perform a needed function, and therefore must be cleared to the level of the system.

8.3.8 Guidance for Similar Cases

Processor/Hardware #4 in this example system warrants additional guidance from that provided above. This hardware set contains partitions running at the same security level with the same recommendation for robustness, with the exception of the Inter-Processor Communication (4Z) partition. The Inter-Processor Communication (4Z) and SRTOS are recommended to be High Robustness assuming that they are maintaining separation of data at different security levels in a Scenario B environment. If however #4 did not require a network connection to the Switch then there would be no Inter-Processor Communication (4Z) partition with possible access to data at different security levels. In this case, Medium Robustness may be appropriate for the SRTOS. Consider a second case where all data passing through the Switch is appropriately encrypted and signed. In this case, Inter-Processor Communications (4Z) should only have access to U data (and encrypted TS, TS//Rel, and S data). It may be reasonable in this case to use a Medium Robustness SRTOS (on only processor #4) and Inter-Processor Communication (4Z). However, since the Medium Robustness Inter-Processor Communication (4Z) will be able to communicate with High Robustness Inter-Processor Communication partitions the issue of the Medium Robustness partition trying to subvert the High Robustness partitions should be addressed.

In this example system there was no means for data to reach an uncleared person and there was no uncleared user. Even the unclassified data sent to the Data Module would be handled as TS since the Data Module also contained TS data. If this example had included an uncleared user, with access limited to unclassified partitions of course, then the guidance for Scenario B would still apply. High Robustness would be appropriate since the highest classification level of the data is Top Secret and the primary risk comes from an authorized but uncleared user. If network connectivity were not limited then the change in risk would result in a recommendation to use the guidance for Scenario D.

73

An example system that would process TS/SCI through Unclassified would need to be compliant with Director of Central Intelligence Directive (DCID) 6/3, likely at Protection Level 5. The guidance for Scenario B would also apply to this situation.

8.4   IA GUIDANCE FOR SCENARIO C

8.4.1   Description of Scenario C

As described in the Environment Scenario section of this report, Scenario C reflects a system having the general characteristics summarized below:

- Physical Security: Security provided by the physical environment of the system is characterized as high risk. For example, the system may be a tactical weapon system that faces a realistic probability of being overrun by an adversary, thus giving the adversary physical access to the system (or a portion of the overall system).

- Types of Users: The system has users within the system that are cleared Secret and some that are not cleared. Users are US users and non-US users.

- Security Domain Levels: The system processes Unclassified and Secret data on a single processor.

- Network Connectivity: The system is connected to significant external networks/systems providing large numbers of remote persons and processes some degree of access to the system. For example, the system may be connected to the NIPRNet, which is connected to the Internet creating an "electronic pathway" for data to flow from anyone on the Internet into the system.

- Applications: The system has broad applications that are in wide use and have known vulnerabilities. An example is a commonly used word processor.

- Protocols and Data Types: The protocols are considered broad. They are in wide use and have known vulnerabilities. An example of a broad protocol is the TCP/IP, which transfers messages. The data types are considered to be open format messages, such as the HTTP Web-based e-mail.

8.4.2   Analysis of Scenario C

Primary areas of risk for Scenario C described above include:

- Physical Security: There is a significant risk that people with physical access to the system may try to subvert the system. Lacking good physical security, an adversary has the opportunity to gain physical access, for example, in an overrun situation.

- Types of Users: There is a significant insider risk posed by the user that is not cleared for Secret information processed by the system. In addition, non-US users pose a risk since they are not cleared for all information processed by the system.

- Security Domain Levels: As the system processes data only at the Secret and Unclassified levels the value of the data is lower than the value of Top Secret data and an adversary would apply fewer resources towards compromising the data.

- Network Connectivity: There is a significant risk posed by the connection to the NIPRNet/Internet. Anyone on the Internet has the opportunity to attack the system. In addition, the connection to the SIPRNet increases the risk since the consequence of a security breach could involve harm to the SIPRNet.

- Applications, Protocols and Data Types: Broadly used applications, protocols and open data types present a significant risk to the system. It is reasonable to expect that known vulnerabilities for these applications, protocols and data types are posted on the Internet and available to any adversary.

8.4.3 Example Scenario C System

An example system based on the characteristics of Scenario C is defined below and depicted in Figure 17.

The example system provides Secret cleared users with fused situational awareness using data from within the system, from SIPRNet, from NIPRNet, and from the Secret Coalition Network (S//Rel). It provides Secret cleared and uncleared users with Web browser access to the NIPRNet and Internet. The system includes a subsystem that can detect certain threats to the platform and respond with countermeasures.

Note that this is only an example of a system that would be consistent with the characteristics for Scenario C. The example system depicted here is only used to illustrate the IA guidance that would be appropriate for any system consistent with the characteristics for Scenario C.

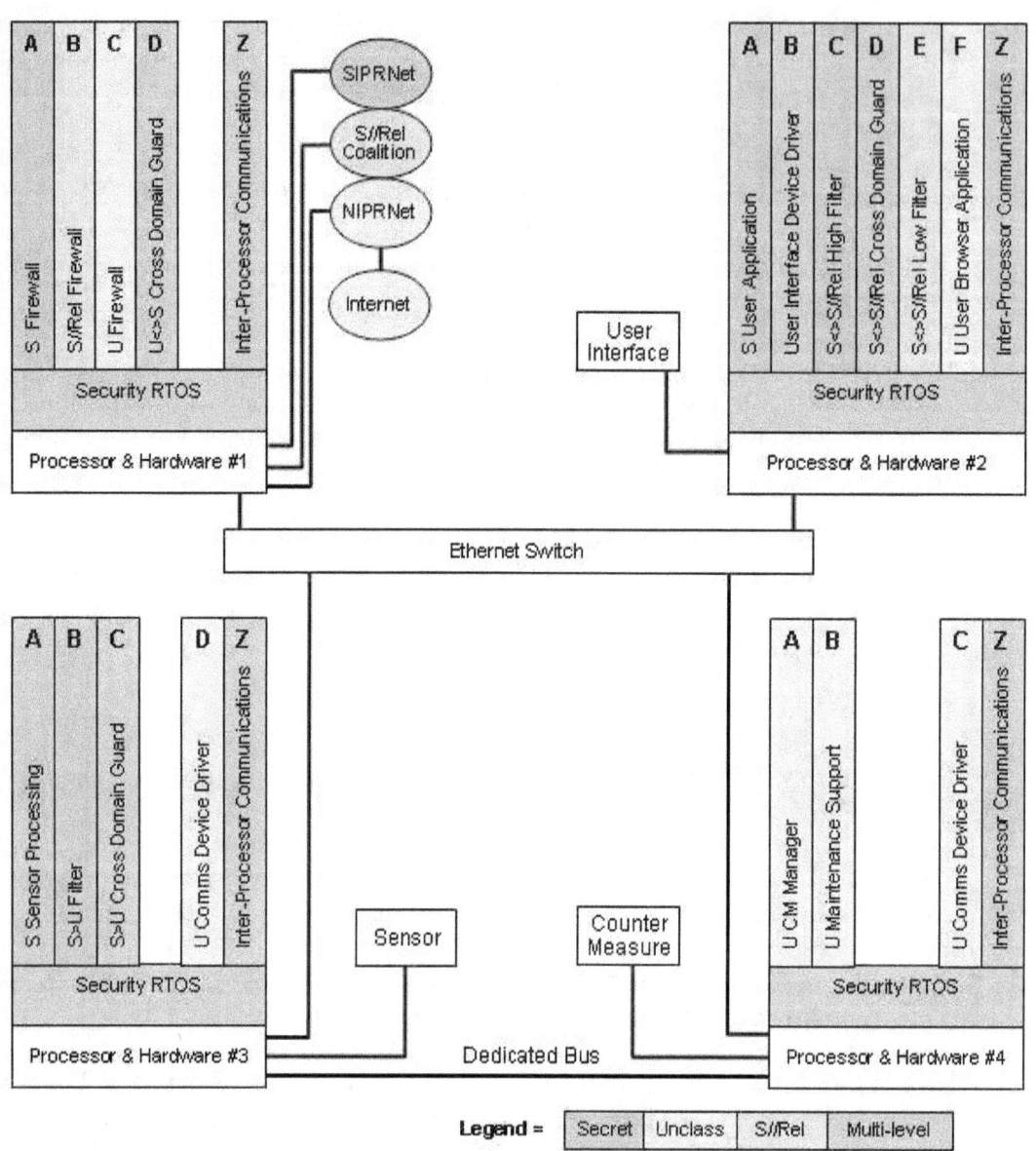

Figure 17: Scenario C

8.4.3.1 COMPONENT DESCRIPTIONS

The following paragraphs describe each of the components in the example system for Scenario C, as depicted in Figure 17. Partitions are represented by the vertical rectangles in the figure, such as "S Sensor Processing." A shorthand notation for referring to a particular partition is used in this document. The shorthand notation is the number for the "Processor & Hardware" hosting the partition and the letter shown in the figure for that partition. For example, U Maintenance Support is a partition on Processor & Hardware #4 and is labeled B, so its shorthand notation is 4B. If a partition involves data and processing at a single classification level then that level is included at the beginning of the name of that partition. For example, the "S" in S Sensor Processing (3A) indicates that this partition only processes Secret data. A "U" is used for unclassified data/processing, An "S" followed by "//Rel" indicates that the data/processing being performed is at some release level (releasable to another nation or set of nations). Partitions that support the movement of data between a partition at one classification level and a partition at a different classification level have two classification levels at the beginning of their name, as well as symbols to denote the direction in which the information flows. For example, the S>U Cross Domain Guard (3C) partition supports the movement of data between a Secret partition (S) and an Unclassified partition (U) with the information flowing from the Secret partition to the Unclassified partition (S>U). If information flows in both directions between the partitions "<>" is used, such as in U<>S Cross Domain Guard (1D).

Processor & Hardware represents the hardware components such as microprocessor, memory (volatile and non-volatile), interface devices, etc. This example system is based on four sets of hardware. This illustrates that most systems will have multiple processors and keeps the number of partitions on any one processor to a reasonable number for discussion. Note that the hardware could be the same for all four sets, but that would require that each set of hardware have all of the necessary interfaces. In particular: Processor & Hardware #1 requires four network interfaces (connection to the Ethernet Switch, connection to NIPRNet, connection to S//Rel Coalition Network, and connection to SIPRNet); Processor & Hardware #2 requires one network interface (connection to the Ethernet Switch) and an interface to the User Interface device (perhaps a touch screen display); Processor & Hardware #3 requires one network interface, a Dedicated Bus interface and an interface to the Sensor; and Processor & Hardware #4 requires one network interface, a Dedicated Bus interface and an interface to the Countermeasure

User Interface represents a Secret (S) device connected to Processor & Hardware #2 that provides a means for the user to interact with the system. It displays situational awareness and other information to the user and it allows the user to enter information for composing situational awareness.

Ethernet Switch represents a device that interconnects the four Processor & Hardware components to allow the exchange of unclassified, Secret, and S//Rel data packets. The Ethernet switch just transfers the packets, and the only decisions it makes are related to the delivery of packets.

Sensor represents a device that monitors the surroundings of the system. It passes Secret information concerning anything it detects to the S Sensor Processing (3A) partition for analysis.

Countermeasure represents a device that deploys a countermeasure to protect the system from a threat detected by the Sensor. It is controlled by the U CM Manager (4A) partition.

Security RTOS represents the SRTOS that fulfills all the characteristics of an SRTOS as described in Section 6, Characteristics of a Security RTOS. It is all the software running in privilege mode on a processor. All other software exists in a partition. Each SRTOS enforces a policy that can control:

- what resources (memory, addresses, etc) are available to a partition (space partitioning)

- the amount of time or processor cycles provided to a partition (time partitioning)

- for a given partition, what other partitions on that processor the given partition can pass information to or receive information from (information flow control).

For example, partition 1A, S Firewall, would be allocated by the SRTOS on Processor & Hardware #1 a portion of the memory/address space available to the processor/SRTOS that would be sufficient for software running in the S Firewall partition. Partition 1A would also be allocated the address(es) necessary for accessing the SIPRNet interface via Processor & Hardware #1. Partition 1A would be allocated a portion of the available processor cycles. Partition 1A would be allowed to receive information from the SIPRNet and send information to partitions such as Inter-Processor Communications (1Z).

S Firewall (1A) represents a partition running at the Secret (S) level that provides firewall services such as filtering to information flowing to or from the SIPRNet.

S//Rel Firewall (1B) represents a partition running at the S//Rel level that provides firewall services such as filtering to information flowing to or from the S//Rel Coalition Network.

U Firewall (1C) represents a partition running at the unclassified (U) level that provides firewall services such as filtering to information flowing to or from the NIPRNet. The NIPRNet is connected to the Internet.

U<>S Cross Domain Guard (1D) represents a partition that performs a cross domain data transfer function. It takes in unclassified data, checks its format, etc, to determine the data is safe and then passes the data to S partitions so that the data can be used in providing situational awareness to the user. It also takes in data from an S partition and verified that the data is unclassified before passing it to a U partition.

Inter-Processor Communications (1Z, 2Z, 3Z, and 4Z) is described in Section 8.6.7. In summary, the four Inter-Processor Communications partitions connect via their respective Processor & Hardware to an Ethernet Switch that they share in common. These partitions support communication between partitions on different processors. Each of the four enforces its own security policy, which are subsets of the overall system security policy. For example, the Inter-Processor Communications (1Z) partition on Processor & Hardware #1 will allow partition S User Application (2A) to communicate with partition S Firewall (1A) but would not allow S User Application (2A) to communicate with partition U CM Manager (4A).

S User Application (2A) represents a partition running at the S level that takes in data from several sources, including the SIPRNet, NIPRNet, S//Rel Coalition network, and user, and fuses/composes a Secret situational awareness picture for the user.

User Interface Device Driver (2B) represents a partition running at the S or U level that handles the interface to the User Interface. It communicates with S User Application (2A) or with U User Browser Application (2F) depending on whether the user is cleared Secret or uncleared and what the user is accessing. It communicates with the User Interface via Processor & Hardware #2.

S<>S//Rel High Filter (2C) represents a partition that performs a subset of the filtering necessary to ensure the flow of S//Rel information up to the S security domain will not harm the S security domain and that only S//Rel information flows from the S security domain to the S//Rel security domain. It works in conjunction with S<>S//Rel Cross Domain Guard (2D) and S<>S//Rel Low Filter (2E).

S<>S//Rel Cross Domain Guard (2D) represents a partition that performs a cross domain data transfer function. It takes in information from the S security domain that has been filtered by S<>S//Rel High Filter (2C), verifies the filtering took place, and passes the S//Rel information to the S<>S//Rel Low Filter (2E). Or it can take in information from the S//Rel security domain that has been filtered by S<>S//Rel Low Filter (2E), verify the filtering took place, and pass the S//Rel information to S<>S//Rel High Filter (2C).

S<>S//Rel Low Filter (2E) represents a partition that performs a subset of the filtering necessary to ensure the flow of S//Rel information up to the S security domain will not harm the S security domain and that only S//Rel information flows from the S security domain to the S//Rel security domain. It works in conjunction with S<>S//Rel High Filter (2C) and S<>S//Rel Cross Domain Guard (2D).

U User Browser Application (2F) represents a partition that provides the user (Secret cleared or uncleared) with Web access to the NIPRNet, and via NIPRNet the Internet. It communicates with the NIPRNet and Internet via the U Firewall (1C).

79

S Sensor Processing (3A) represents a partition running at the Secret level that takes in Secret data from the Sensor device and analyzes that data. If S Sensor Processing (3A) detects an immediate threat to the system (perhaps a missile coming towards a fighter plane) then it can initiate an action to respond with a Countermeasure (perhaps releasing chaff from the fighter plane to confuse the missile). S Sensor Processing (3A) also provides its Secret analysis of the data from the Sensor device to the partition S User Application (3A) where that data is used to compose the Secret situational awareness for the user.

S>U Filter (3B) represents a partition that performs a data filtering function. It takes in a command to respond with a Countermeasure from the partition S Sensor Processing (3A), verifies the data is unclassified, etc, and then passes the command to the S>U Cross Domain Guard (3C). It works in conjunction with S>U Cross Domain Guard (3C).

S>U Cross Domain Guard (3C) represents a partition that performs a cross domain data transfer function. It takes in a command to respond with a Countermeasure from S>U Filter (3B), verifies the filtering was performed, and then passes the command to U CM Manager (4A).

U Comms Device Driver (3D and 4C) represents a partition running at the unclassified level that handles the interface to the Dedicated Bus. This partition exists separately on both Processor & Hardware #3 and Processor & Hardware #4.

Dedicated Bus represents a dedicated serial data bus that transfers information from Processor & Hardware #3 to Processor & Hardware #4. It is used to transfer the command to initiate a Countermeasure from Processor & Hardware #3 to Processor & Hardware #4. The Dedicated Bus interface on Processor & Hardware #3 can only be accessed by the U Comms Device Driver (3D) partition, a policy enforced by the SRTOS. The Dedicated Bus interface on Processor & Hardware #4 can only be accessed by the U Comms Device Driver (4C) partition, a policy enforced by the SRTOS.

U CM Manager (4A) represents a partition running at the unclassified level that controls the Countermeasure device and tracks usage of the Countermeasure. It reports usage of the Countermeasure to the U Maintenance Support (4B) partition.

U Maintenance Support (4B) represents a partition running at the unclassified level that receives information on the expenditure of Countermeasures and tracks Countermeasure usage. When replenishment of the Countermeasure is necessary the U Maintenance Support (4B) partition can send this fact to the appropriate organization via the NIPRNet.

8.4.3.2 DETECT AND RESPOND

If processing/analyzing of sensor data by S Sensor Processing (3A, processor/hardware #3 partition A) identifies an immediate threat S Sensor Processing (3A) sends a command to take appropriate countermeasure (CM) to the U CM Manager (4A). Since the command is originating in a S partition and going to a U partition it must pass through a cross domain guard.

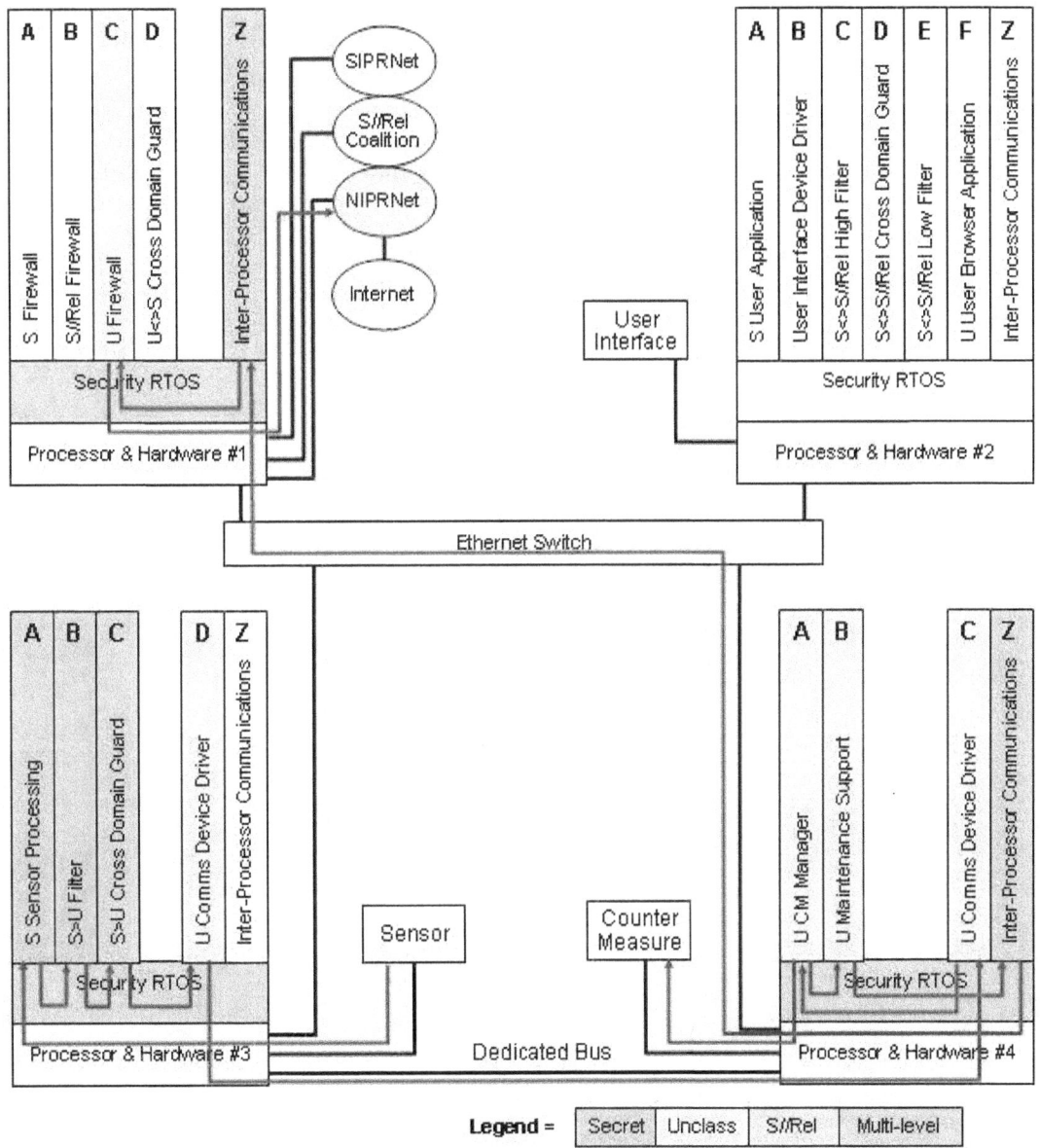

Figure 18: Scenario C Detect and Respond

- The command is passed from S Sensor Processing (3A) to S>U Filter (3B) where the data is examined to ensure no S data is present.

- It is passed from S>U Filter (3B) to S>U Cross Domain Guard (3C) where the data is checked and regraded as U.

81

- From S>U Cross Domain Guard (3C) the command is passed via the U Communications Device Drivers (3D and 4C) and a Dedicated Bus

- to U CM Manager (4A).

The Dedicated Bus is necessary to preserve the real time determinism required between Sensor and Countermeasure. After receiving the command, U CM Manager (4A) sends an instruction to Countermeasure that deploys a countermeasure to the imminent threat detected by the Sensor.

The U CM Manager (4A) reports to U Maintenance Support (4B) that it has expended a countermeasure so the system knows it will need to be replaced at the next opportunity. U Maintenance Support (4B) passes the information to a logistics database on the NIPRNet so that plans can be put in place to replenish the expended countermeasure.

- The information passes from U Maintenance Support (4B) via the Inter-Processor Communications (4Z and 1Z)

- to the U Firewall (1C)

- and then to the NIPRNet.

Data sent to NIPRNet should have appropriate protections for confidentiality and integrity applied.

8.4.3.3 FUSED SITUATIONAL AWARENESS

To maintain complete situational awareness (SA) S User Application (2A) receives information from the system's Sensor but also from SIPRNET, the S//Rel Coalition Network, and the NIPRNet.

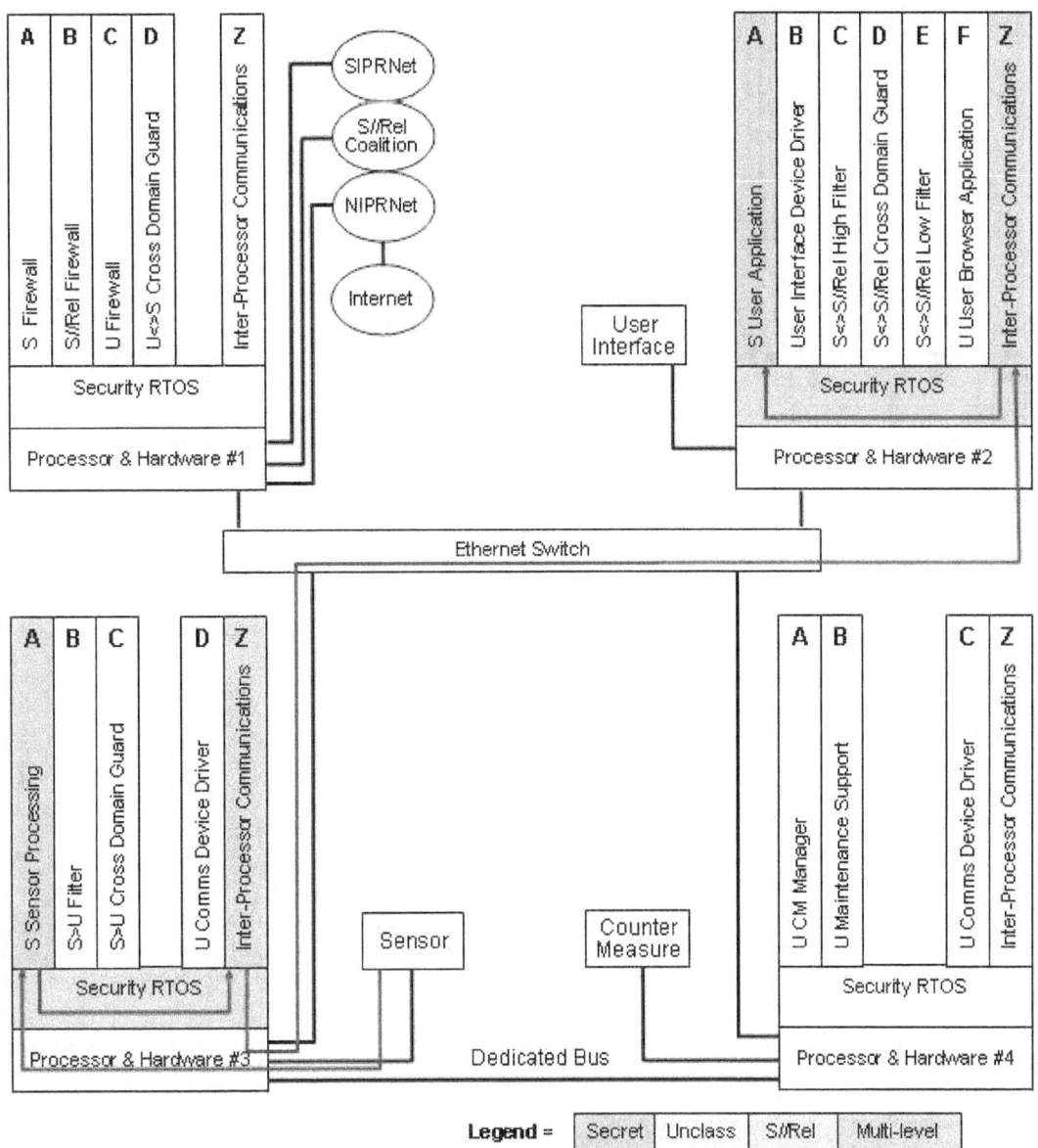

Figure 19: Scenario C SA Data From Sensor

One input that is used to create situational awareness for the user is generated by the Sensor. The Sensor outputs Secret data to S Sensor Processing (3A) where the data is processed/analyzed and then fed into the user's SA (S User Application, 2A).

- Data moves from the Sensor to S Sensor Processing (3A) which provides its analysis of the data

- via Inter-Processor Communications (3Z and 2Z)

- to S User Application (2A).

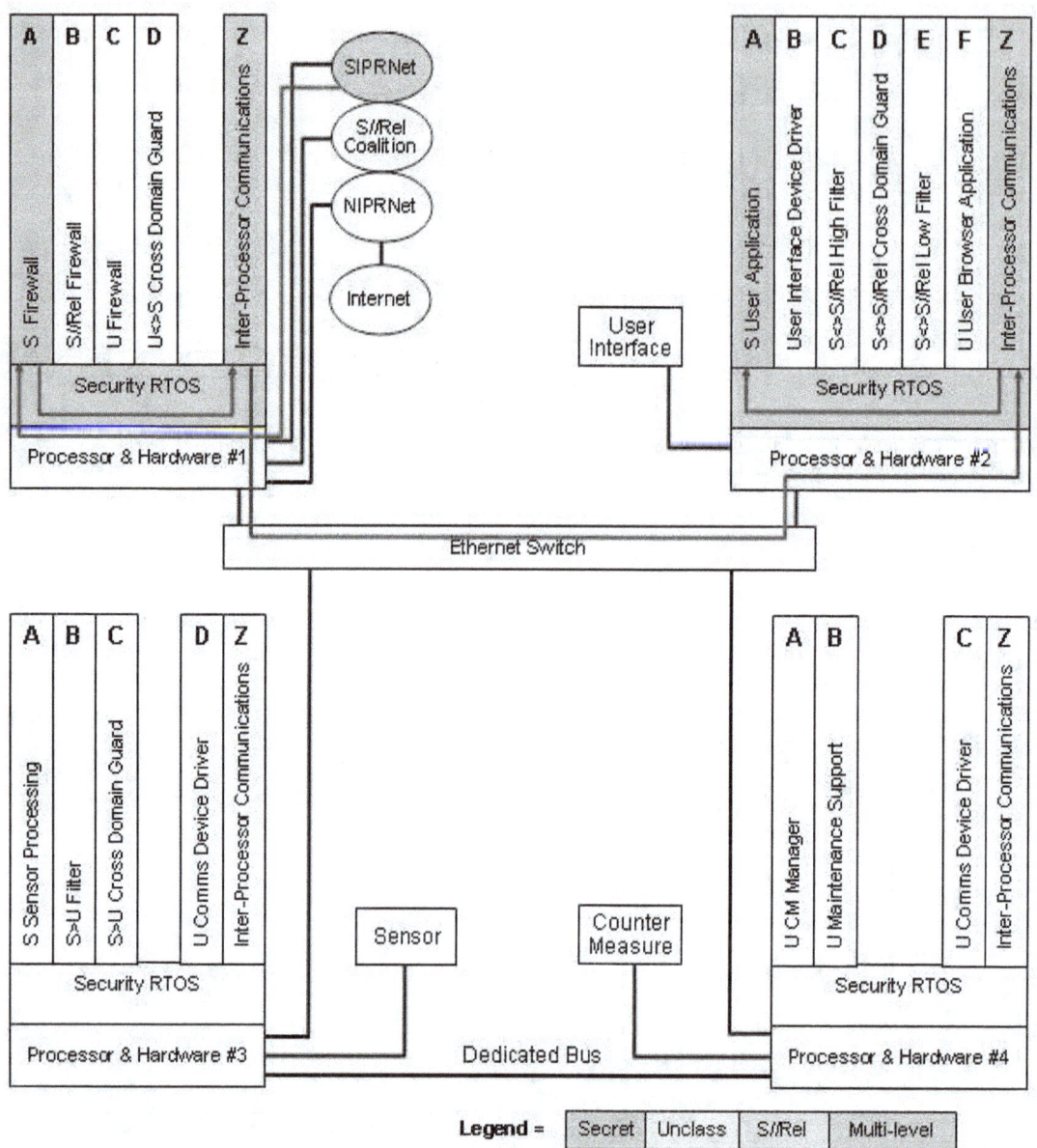

Figure 20: Scenario C SA Data From SIPRNet

Additional SA information is received by S Sensor Processing (3A) from the SIPRNet.

- SA data from SIPRNet is passed through the S Firewall (1A) and then

- via the Inter-Processor Communications (1Z and 2Z)

- to S User Application (2A).

SA data being received from the S//Rel Coalition Network must pass through a cross domain guard to get to the S User Application (2A).

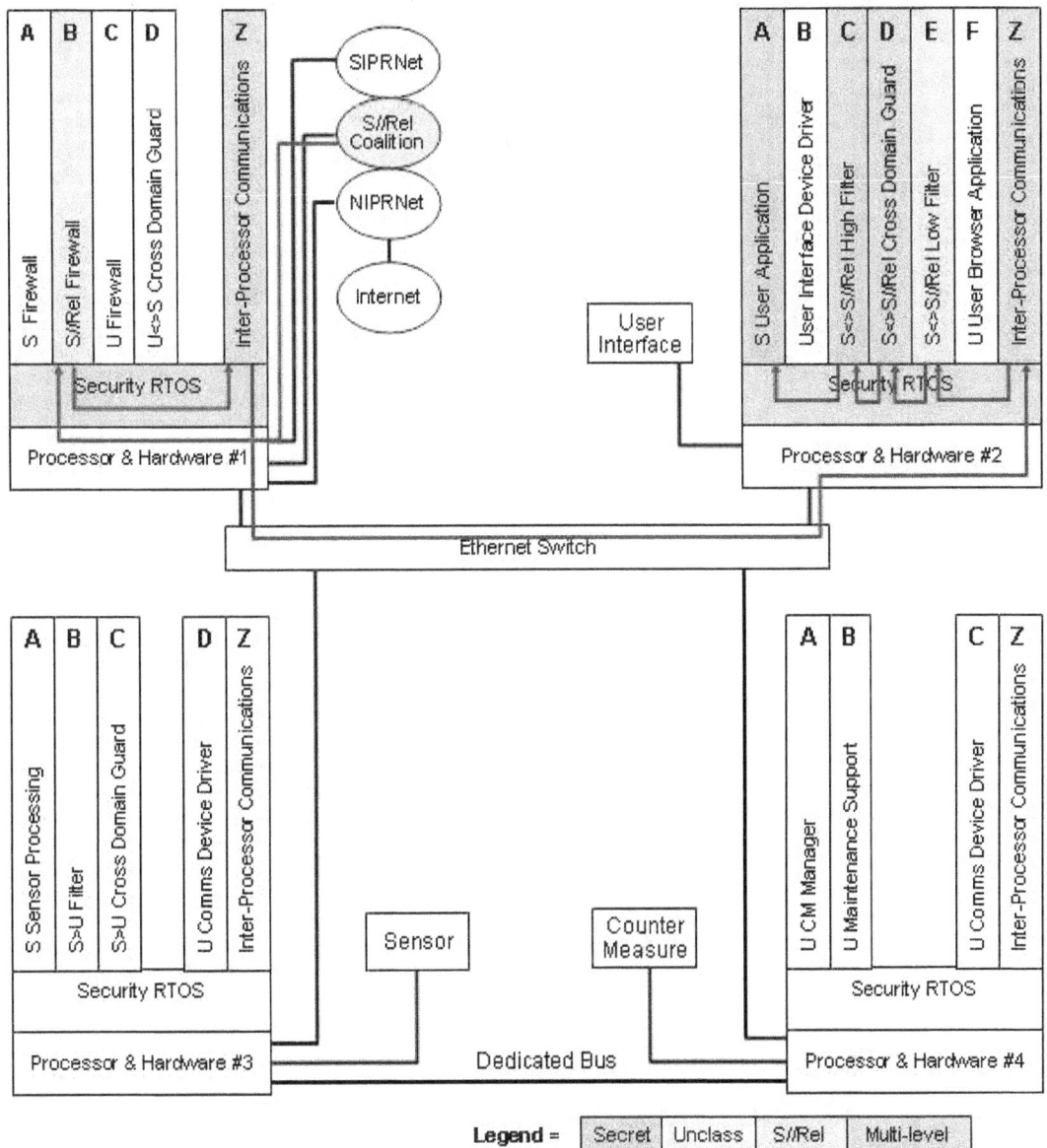

Figure 21: Scenario C SA Data From S/Rel Coalition Network

- Data from S//Rel Coalition Network passes through the S//Rel Firewall (1B) and then,

- via Inter-Processor Communications (1Z and 2Z),

- to the S<>S//Rel Low Filter (2E) where it is filtered and

- passed to the S<>S//Rel Cross Domain Guard (2D) where it is checked and regraded to S and

- sent to the S<>S//Rel High Filter (2C) which ensures it is not harmful and passes it

- to S User Application (2A).

In addition to SA data from SIPRNet and the S//Rel Coalition Network, S User Application (2A) also receives weather data from the NIPRNet.

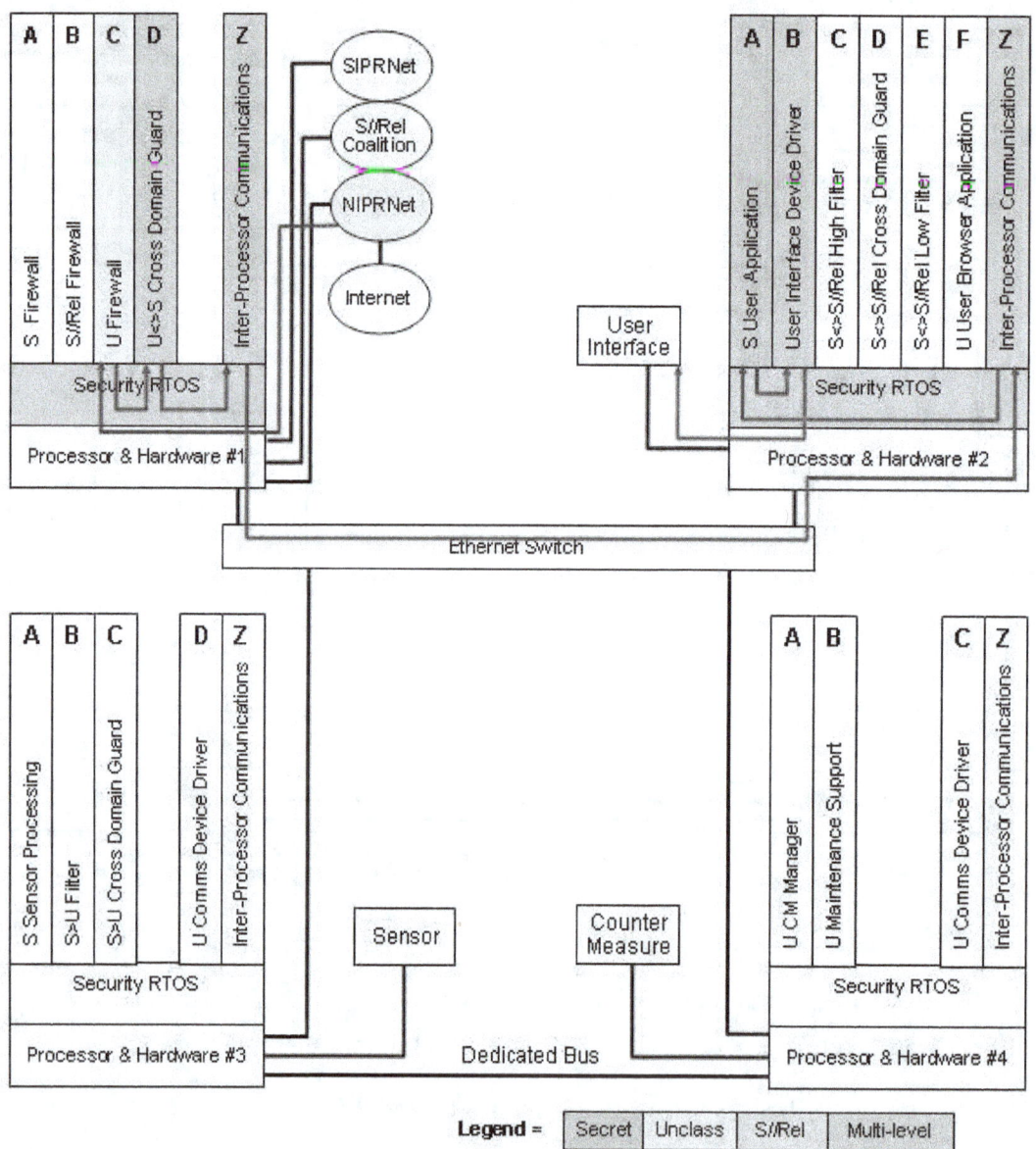

Figure 22: Scenario C Weather Data From NIPRNet

- The weather data from the NIPRNet is passed to the U Firewall (1C) and then

- to the U<>S Cross Domain Guard (1D) which regrades the data to S and sends it

- via the Inter-Processor Communication System (1Z and 2Z)

- to S User Application (2A).

The U◇S Cross Domain Guard (1D) ensures only harmless weather data is passed to S User Application (2A). S User Application (2A) fuses all the data it has received and provides SA to the Secret User via the User Interface. S User Application (2A) interfaces with the User Interface via the User Interface Device Driver (2B).

8.4.3.4 REPORTING SITUATIONAL AWARENESS AND STATUS

S User Application (2A) is also responsible for providing appropriate fused SA to the SIPRNet, a sanitized version of the SA to the S//Rel Coalition Network, and status information to the NIPRNet.

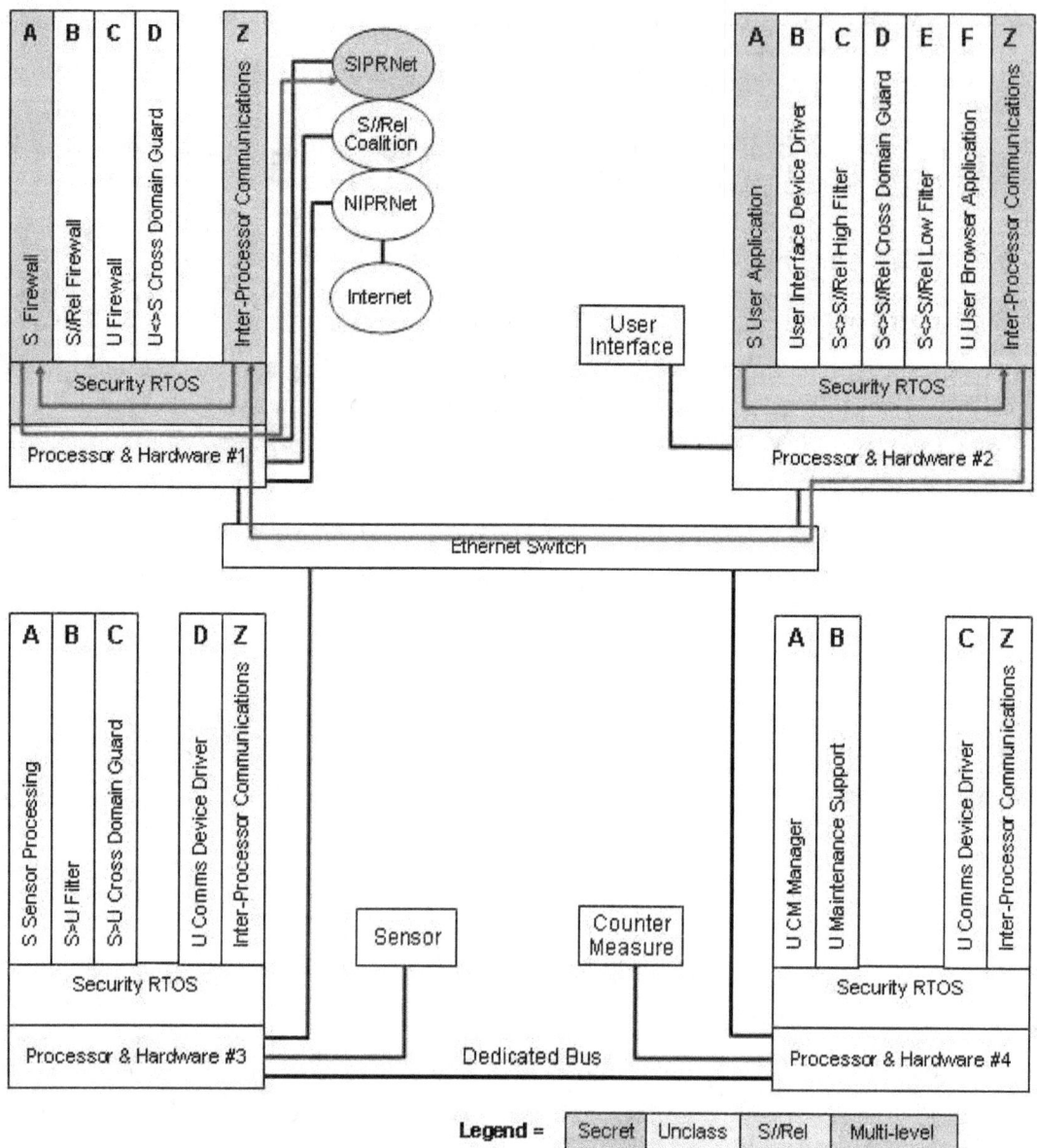

Figure 23: Scenario C Fused SA To SIPRNet

- S User Application (2A) passes fused SA data

- via Inter-Processor Communications (2Z and 1Z)

- to the S Firewall (1A) which sends it

- to the SIPRNet.

S User Application (2A) also sends fused SA to the S//Rel Coalition Network, but the data must be sanitized before it is released to the S//Rel Coalition Network.

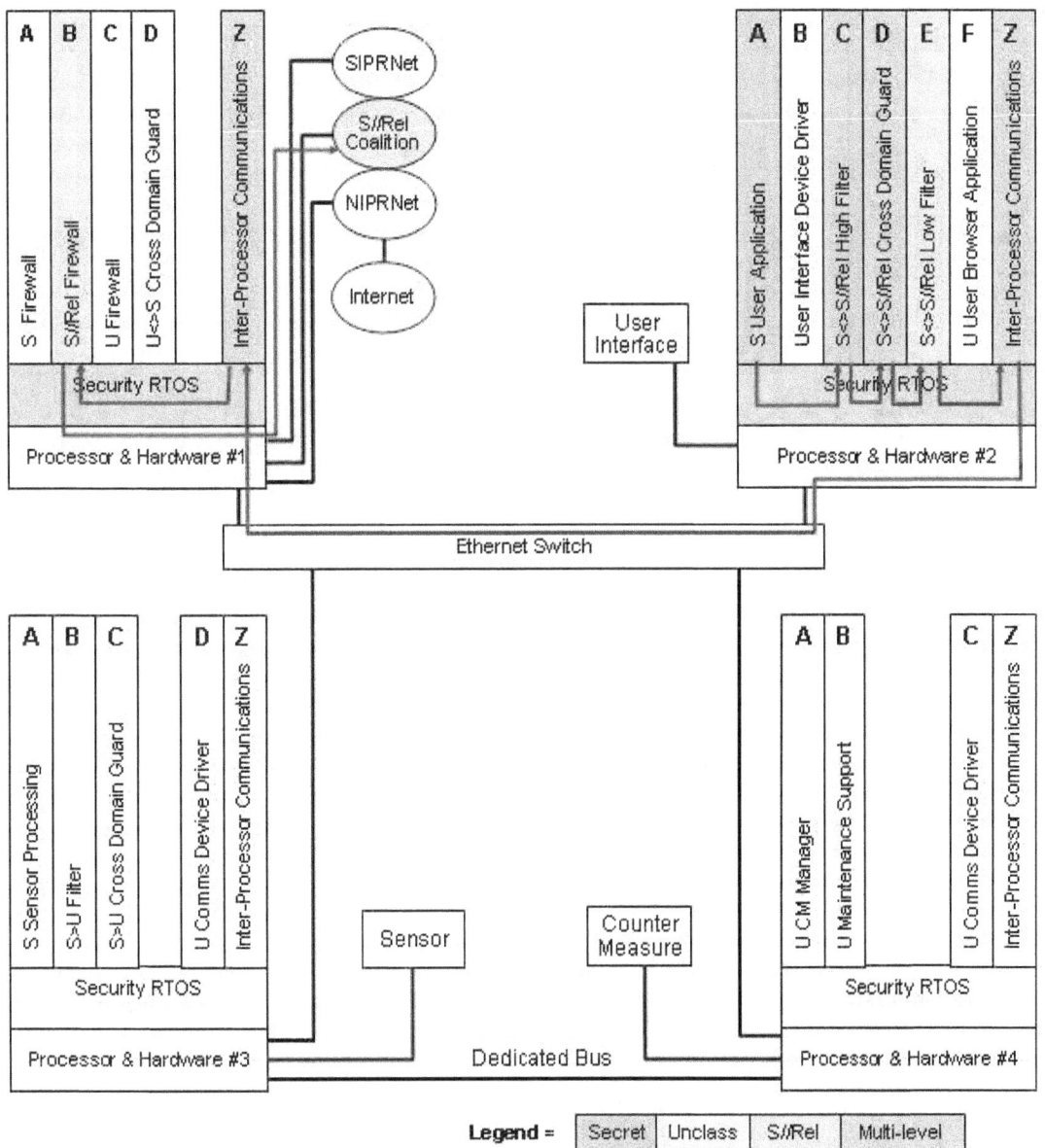

Figure 24: Scenario C Sanitized SA To S//Rel Coalition Network

- S User Application (2A) passes fused SA data

- via S<>S//Rel High Filter (2C)

- and S<>S//Rel Cross Domain Guard (2D)

- to the S<>S//Rel Low Filter (2E) and

- via the Inter-Processor Communications (2Z and 1Z)

89

- and the S//Rel Firewall (1B)

- to the S//Rel Coalition Network.

S<>S//Rel High Filter (2C), S<>S//Rel Cross Domain Guard (2D), and S<>S//Rel Low Filter (2E) sanitize and regrade to S//Rel the SA information so it is appropriate for release to the S//Rel Coalition Network.

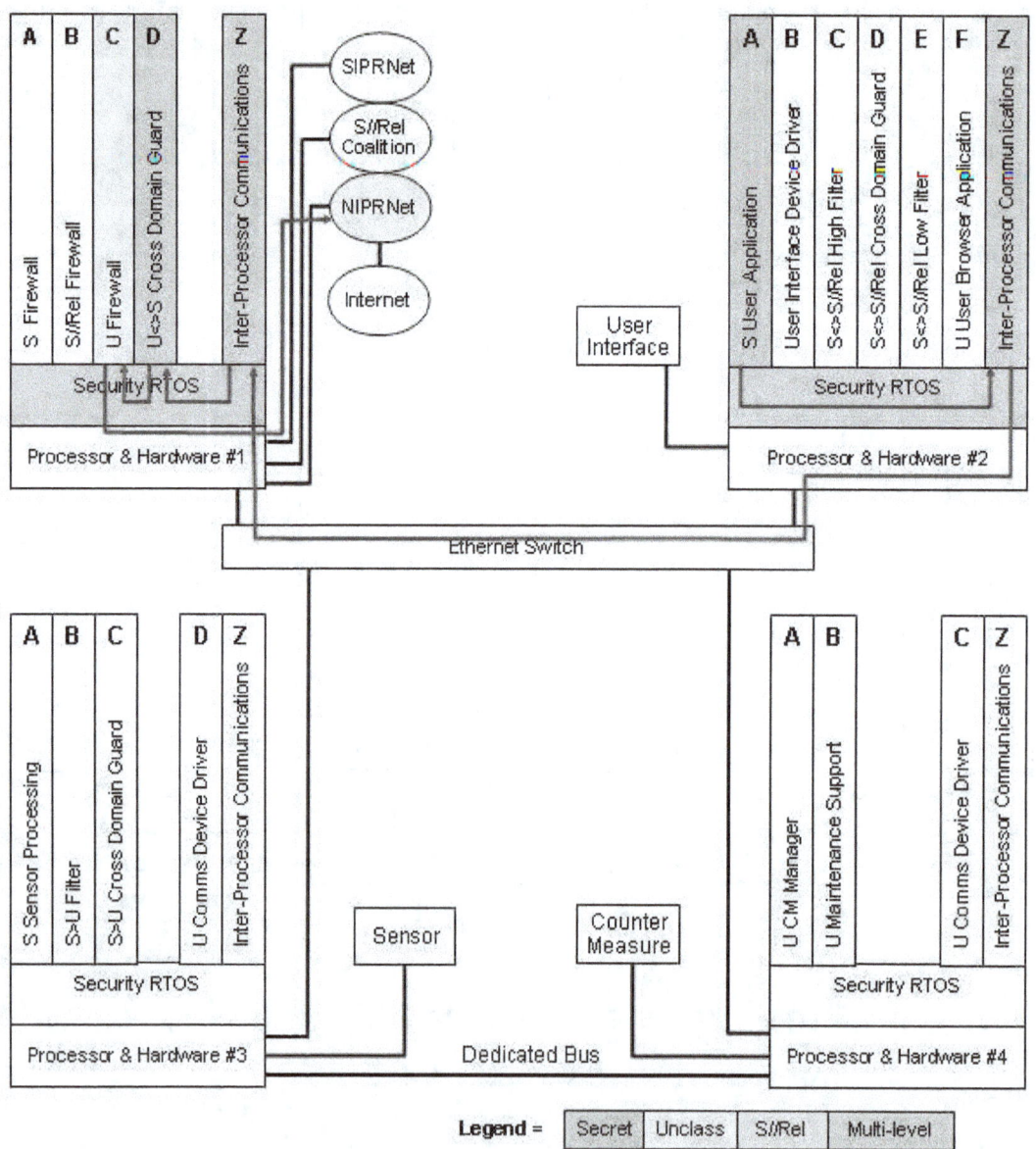

Figure 25: Scenario C Basic Status Information to NIPRNet

S User Application (2A) provides basic status information to the NIPRNet.

- S User Application (2A) sends the basic status information

90

- via the Inter-Processor Communications (2Z and 1Z)

- to the U<>S Cross Domain Guard (1D) and

- the U Firewall (1C)

- to the NIPRNet.

The U<>S Cross Domain Guard ensures that only fixed formatted status messages are sent from S User Application (2A) to the NIPRNet and the data contains no classified information. Data sent to NIPRNet should have appropriate protections for confidentiality and integrity applied.

8.4.3.5 WEB BROWSING

U User Browser Application (2F) provides users with a Web browser application for accessing the NIPRNet and Internet for Computer Based Training, knowledge portals, etc.

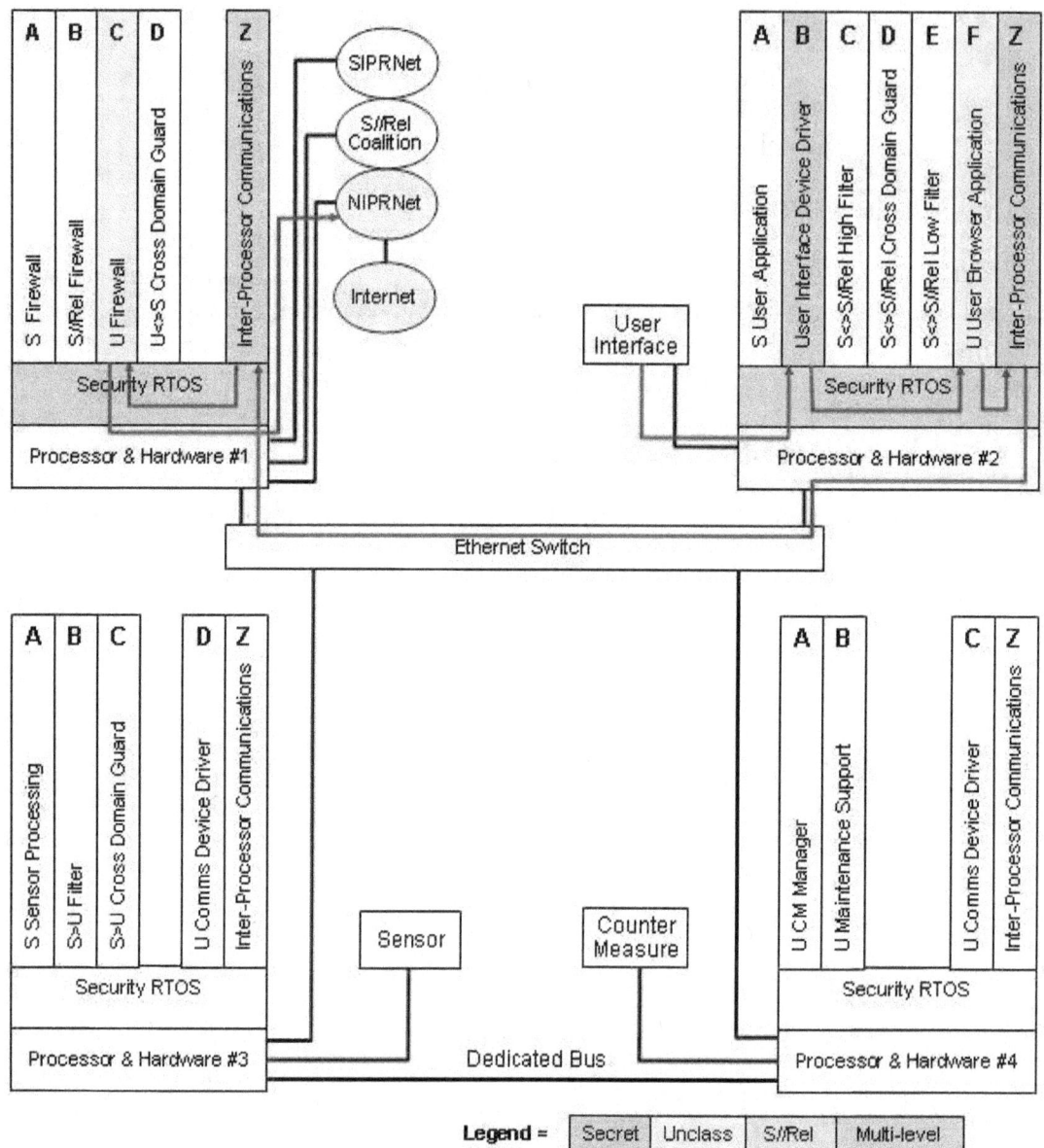

Figure 26: Scenario C Web Browsing Capability

- U User Browser Application (2F) communicates

- via Inter-Processor Communications (2Z and 1Z)

- and the U Firewall (1C)

- with the NIPRNet and Internet.

U User Browser Application (2F) interacts with the User via the User Interface Device Driver (2B) and User Interface.

8.4.3.6 INFORMATION FLOW CONTROL POLICY

Several of the components in Figure 17 are responsible for enforcing security policies pertaining to information flow. The information flow control policy for each of those components is described below.

The Security RTOS (SRTOS) on Processor & Hardware #1 enforces an information flow control policy between the partitions running on Processor & Hardware #1 and between those partitions and the resources associated with Processor & Hardware #1 that are under the control of the SRTOS. The information flow control policy enforced by the SRTOS on Processor & Hardware #1 is as follows. All other information flows are not permitted by the SRTOS.

- S Firewall (1A) can send and receive information to/from the SIPRNet

- S Firewall (1A) can send and receive information to/from Inter-Processor Communications (1Z)

- S//Rel Firewall (1B) can send and receive information to/from the S//Rel Coalition Network

- S//Rel Firewall (1B) can send and receive information to/from Inter-Processor Communications (1Z)

- U Firewall (1C) can send and receive information to/from the NIPRNet

- U Firewall (1C) can send and receive information to/from U<>S Cross Domain Guard (1D)

- U Firewall (1C) can send and receive information to/from Inter-Processor Communications (1Z)

- U<>S Cross Domain Guard (1D) can send and receive information to/from Inter-Processor Communications (1Z)

- Inter-Processor Communications (1Z) can send and receive information to/from the Ethernet Switch

Inter-Processor Communications (1Z) enforces an information flow control policy between the partitions running on Processor & Hardware #1 and partitions running on any of the other three Processor & Hardware components. The information flow control policy enforced by Inter-Processor Communications (1Z) is as follows. All other information flows are not permitted by Inter-Processor Communications (1Z).

- S Firewall (1A) can send and receive information to/from S User Application (2A)

93

- S//Rel Firewall (1B) can send and receive information to/from S<>S//Rel Low Filter (2E)

- U Firewall (1C) can send and receive information to/from U User Browser Application (2F)

- U<>S Cross Domain Guard (1D) can send and receive information to/from S User Application (2A)

U<>S Cross Domain Guard (1D) enforces an information flow control policy between partitions running in one security domain (classification level in the example) and partitions running in a different security domain (classification level in the example). The information flow control policy enforced by U<>S Cross Domain Guard (1D) is as follows. All other information flows are not permitted U<>S Cross Domain Guard (1D).

- U Firewall (1C) can send and receive information to/from S User Application (2A)

The Security RTOS (SRTOS) on Processor & Hardware #2 enforces an information flow control policy between the partitions running on Processor & Hardware #2 and between those partitions and the resources associated with Processor & Hardware #2 that are under the control of the SRTOS. The information flow control policy enforced by the SRTOS on Processor & Hardware #2 is as follows. All other information flows are not permitted by the SRTOS.

- S User Application (2A) can send and receive information to/from User Interface Device Driver (2B)

- S User Application (2A) can send and receive information to/from S<>S//Rel High Filter (2C)

- S User Application (2A) can send and receive information to/from Inter-Processor Communications (2Z)

- User Interface Device Driver (2B) can send and receive information to/from the User Interface

- S<>S//Rel High Filter (2C) can send and receive information to/from S<>S//Rel Cross Domain Guard (2D)

- S<>S//Rel Cross Domain Guard (2D) can send and receive information to/from S<>S//Rel Low Filter (2E)

- U User Browser Application (2F) can send and receive information to/from User Interface Device Driver (2B)

- U User Browser Application (2F) can receive information from Inter-Processor Communications (2Z)

94

- Inter-Processor Communications (2Z) can send and receive information to/from the Ethernet Switch

Inter-Processor Communications (2Z) enforces an information flow control policy between the partitions running on Processor & Hardware #2 and partitions running on any of the other three Processor & Hardware components. The information flow control policy enforced by Inter-Processor Communications (2Z) is as follows. All other information flows are not permitted by Inter-Processor Communications (2Z).

- S User Application (2A) can send and receive information to/from S Firewall (1A)

- S User Application (2A) can send and receive information to/from U<>S Cross Domain Guard (1D)

- S User Application (2A) can receive information from S Sensor Processing (3A)

- S<>S//Rel Low Filter (2E) can send and receive information to/from S//Rel Firewall (1B)

- U User Browser Application (2F) can send and receive information to/from U Firewall (1C)

S<>S//Rel Cross Domain Guard (2D) enforces an information flow control policy between partitions running in one security domain (classification level in the example) and partitions running in a different security domain (classification level in the example). The information flow control policy enforced by S<>S//Rel Cross Domain Guard (2D) is as follows. All other information flows are not permitted by S<>S//Rel Cross Domain Guard (2D).

- S//Rel Firewall (1B) can send and receive information to/from S User Application (2A)

The Security RTOS (SRTOS) on Processor & Hardware #3 enforces an information flow control policy between the partitions running on Processor & Hardware #3 and between those partitions and the resources associated with Processor & Hardware #3 that are under the control of the SRTOS. The information flow control policy enforced by the SRTOS on Processor & Hardware #3 is as follows. All other information flows are not permitted by the SRTOS.

- S Sensor Processing (3A) can receive information from the Sensor

- S Sensor Processing (3A) can send information to S>U Filter (3B)

- S Sensor Processing (3A) can send information to Inter-Processor Communications (3Z)

95

- S>U Filter (3B) can send information to S>U Cross Domain Guard (3C)

- S>U Cross Domain Guard (3C) can send information to U Comms Device Driver (3D)

- U Comms Device Driver (3D) can send information to/via the Dedicated Bus

- Inter-Processor Communications (3Z) can send and receive information to/from the Ethernet Switch

Inter-Processor Communications (3Z) enforces an information flow control policy between the partitions running on Processor & Hardware #3 and partitions running on any of the other three Processor & Hardware components. The information flow control policy enforced by Inter-Processor Communications (3Z) is as follows. All other information flows are not permitted by Inter-Processor Communications (3Z).

- S Sensor Processing (3A) can send information to S User Application (2A)

- S>U Cross Domain Guard (3C) can send information to U CM Manager (4A)

S>U Cross Domain Guard (3C) enforces an information flow control policy between partitions running in one security domain (classification level in the example) and partitions running in a different security domain (classification level in the example). The information flow control policy enforced by S>U Cross Domain Guard (3C) is as follows. All other information flows are not permitted by S>U Cross Domain Guard (3C).

- S Sensor Processing (3A) can send information to U CM Manager (4A)

The Security RTOS (SRTOS) on Processor & Hardware #4 enforces an information flow control policy between the partitions running on Processor & Hardware #4 and between those partitions and the resources associated with Processor & Hardware #4 that are under the control of the SRTOS. The information flow control policy enforced by the SRTOS on Processor & Hardware #4 is as follows. All other information flows are not permitted by the SRTOS.

- U CM Manager (4A) can receive information from U Comms Device Driver (4C)

- U CM Manager (4A) can send and receive information to/from the Countermeasure

- U CM Manager (4A) can send information to U Maintenance Support (4B)

- U Maintenance Support (4B) can send information to Inter-Processor Communications (4Z)

- U Comms Device Driver (4C) can receive information from the Dedicated Bus

- Inter-Processor Communications (4Z) can send and receive information to/from the Ethernet Switch

Inter-Processor Communications (4Z) enforces an information flow control policy between the partitions running on Processor & Hardware #4 and partitions running on any of the other three Processor & Hardware components. The information flow control policy enforced by Inter-Processor Communications (4Z) is as follows. All other information flows are not permitted by Inter-Processor Communications (4Z).

- U Maintenance Support (4B) can send information to U Firewall (1C)

8.4.4 Component Robustness Level Guidance

The recommended assurance robustness levels for components within the Scenario C example system are shown in the table below and depicted in Figure 27.

Category	Robustness Level	Components
RTOS	High Robustness	SRTOS
Inter-Processor Communications	High Robustness	Inter-Processor Communications
Single-Level Applications	Basic Robustness or higher	S User Application U User Browser Application S Sensor Processing U CM Manager U Maintenance Support
Single-Level COTS IA Applications	Medium Robustness	U Firewall S Firewall S//Rel Firewall
Multi-Level Device Drivers	High Robustness	User Interface Device Driver
Single-Level Device Drivers	Basic Robustness or higher	U Comms Device Driver
Cross Domain Guards	High Robustness	U<>S Cross Domain Guard
Cross Domain Guards	Medium Robustness	S<>S//Rel High Filter and S<>S//Rel Cross Domain Guard and S<>S//Rel Low Filter S>U Filter and S>U Cross Domain Guard

Table 10: Scenario C Recommended Component Robustness Levels

The components for which High Robustness is recommended are all components where a failure within that component alone could result in the compromise of classified data (a breach in confidentiality). High Robustness is appropriate for this scenario since the highest classification of the data is Secret, not all users are cleared for all the data in the system, and there is a significant threat to the system via the NIPRNet/Internet connectivity. Basic or Medium Robustness for these components would provide inadequate confidence that a breach in confidentiality would not occur. The following table describes the component, its security function, and the consequence of the component failing to perform its security function.

Component	Function	Failure Consequence
SRTOS	Provides partition isolation and information flow control between partitions on a processor	Its failure could result in Secret data being available to an Unclassified process or user
Inter-Processor Communication (1Z, 2Z, 3Z, 4Z) and Switch	Receives Secret and Unclassified data on one processor and delivers that data to Secret and Unclassified partitions on another processor	Its failure could result in Secret data being available to an Unclassified process or user
User Interface Device Driver (2B)	Controls interactions with Secret cleared users and uncleared users via the User Interface and has access to both Secret data from the S User Application (2A) partition and unclassified data from the U User Browser Application (2F) partition	Its failure could result in Secret data being available to an uncleared user or unclassified process
U<>S Cross Domain Guard (1D)	Passes data in both directions between Unclassified and Secret partitions	Its failure could result in the compromise of classified data

Table 11: Consequence of Component Failure

To successfully be evaluated at a High Robustness level the size and complexity of a component must be reasonably small. At present, expectations are that an RTOS, Inter-Processor Communication, and some cross domain guards (such as the one in partition 1D) can achieve High Robustness. However, some cross domain guards will likely not be able to achieve High Robustness. In cases such as this the guidance below applies.

The components for which Medium Robustness is recommended are either IA components performing a critical security function to protect the system from external networks while allowing the flow of appropriate data or critical components of a distributed cross domain guard. For the former this includes the U Firewall (1C), S//Rel Firewall (1B) and S Firewall (1A). The failure of any of these firewalls would allow a very large number of external network users to gain inappropriate access to processes and data at the same classification level within the system depicted by Scenario C. The Protection Profile for firewalls in medium robustness environments should be considered. Since the inappropriate access is to processes and data at the same classification level High Robustness would typically not be warranted.

If the requirement is for the one-way transfer of data from Unclassified to Secret or from Secret to Unclassified, a Medium Robustness cross domain guard could be used if a complementary Medium Robustness security filtering application is implemented on the Secret side of the cross domain guard in a separate partition. This is depicted by the S>U Filter (3B) and S>U Cross Domain Guard (3C) partitions. Since a one-way transfer of data basically limits an adversary to attempting to install malicious code (via a low-to-high data transfer), or to obtaining classified data only when an error is made on the high side (inadvertent disclosure via a high-to-low data transfer), it may be sufficient to implement appropriate filtering and guarding functions at Medium Robustness in a complementary manner. Note that the filter component should always be at the highest security level irrespective of whether the data is flowing from the higher security level to a lower level or lower security level to higher level.

If the requirement is for the bidirectional transfer of data between Unclassified and Secret a Medium Robustness cross domain guard could be used if complementary Medium Robustness security filtering applications are implemented on the Secret side of the cross domain guard and on the Unclassified side of the cross domain guard in separate partitions. This is depicted by the S<>S//Rel High Filter (2C), S<>S//Rel Cross Domain Guard (2D), and the S<>S//Rel Low Filter (2E) partitions in Scenario C.

The layering of independent but complementary security functions/checks in multiple partitions can often be used to reduce the robustness level of any one component. An analogy in cryptography would be triple Data Encryption Standard (DES). Triple DES uses three independent and complementary instantiations of DES. While an adversary may have the resources to determine the underlying data if it is protected by DES, layering in the manner used for triple DES dramatically increases the adversary's cost and so long as that cost is then higher than the adversary is willing or able to pay then adequate protection is achieved. In this example system a similar approach is described for implementing a cross domain solution comprised of multiple Medium Robustness components, hence causing the adversary's cost to increase since each component would need to be subverted. A similar approach could be used for the Inter-Processor Communications. If the Inter-Processor Communications (IPC) partition was divided into two independent security functions/partitions, one checking data received and one checking data sent, then an adversary would need to subvert/defeat both the "transmit" IPC and the "receive" IPC in order to pass unauthorized data from one processor to another. If the transmit and receive components did not share a common flaw then the adversary must expend resources to find two complementary flaws. It is possible then that the transmit and receive components could be at Medium Robustness and provide adequate protection. When using this layering approach it is important that the partitions be independent (the same flaw is unlikely to exist in both) and complementary (a security breach requires breaching all of the layers). It would likely be impractical to apply this approach to the SRTOS.

Although S and S//Rel may appear to be at the same security level they should be considered as different security levels since not all parties hold the same clearance (US users hold a US Secret clearance, Nation X users hold a Nation X Secret clearance). This is different than compartmented/SAR/SAP data protection where all users hold the same US clearance but some have not been granted formal access approval to the compartmented/SAR/SAP data.

Since a bidirectional transfer of data basically gives an adversary the opportunity to install malicious code (via a low-to-high data transfer) and then obtain unauthorized data (via a high-to-low data transfer) a thorough and complementary implementation of security mechanisms across all three partitions at Medium Robustness may be sufficient.

In cases where the cross domain guard is interconnecting S and S//Rel environments the threat represented by the coalition or ally can be used as a factor in determining the capabilities and assurance of the cross domain guard and filters. If the S//Rel environment is highly trusted then there is less risk that it will attempt to subvert the S environment and appropriate trade-offs can be made on data types permitted to traverse the cross domain guard and the assurance level of the cross domain guard. Even for most trusted allies an assurance level of at least EAL 4 is recommended.

The components for which Basic Robustness is recommended are all components that are at a low risk of compromising data (breaching confidentiality) but do provide integrity and availability for the system. Basic Robustness is the minimum level recommended for these components. S User Application (2A), U User Browser Application (2F), S Sensor Processing (3A) U CM Manager (4A), U Maintenance Support (4B), and U Communications Device Driver (3D and 4C) perform important mission functions and could breach integrity or availability but not confidentiality. In some cases, Medium Robustness or other increases beyond Basic Robustness may be appropriate for addressing privacy, availability, integrity and other concerns.

If a Protection Profile exists for any component at the appropriate robustness level compliance with that Protection Profile should be strongly considered as a requirement for that component.

The Ethernet Switch component is potentially a special case and is discussed in detail in Section 8.6.8.

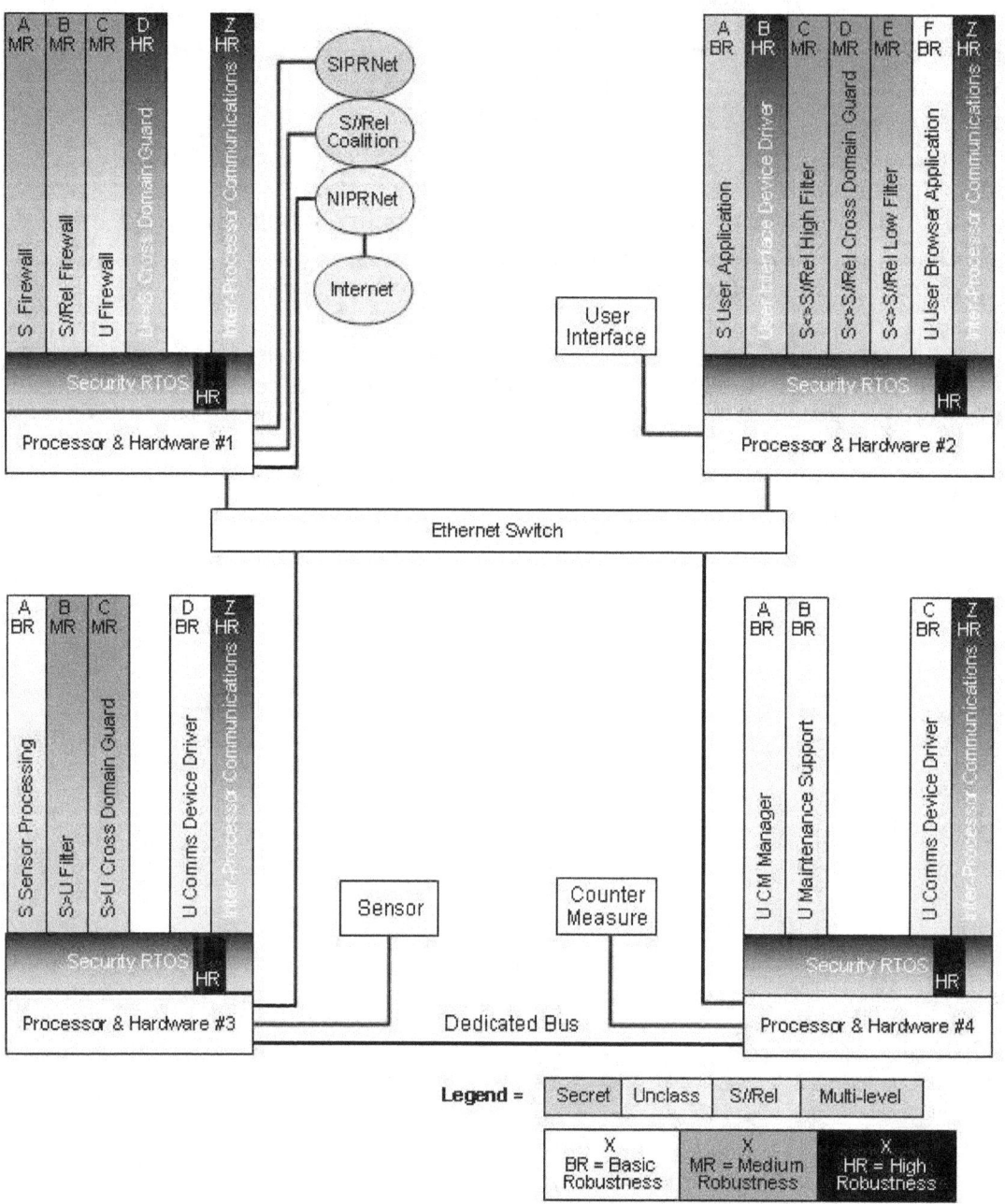

Figure 27: Scenario C Component Robustness Levels

8.4.5 Covert Channel Analysis Guidance

The purpose of the covert channel analysis is to identify and quantify covert channels and the associated residual risk. Covert channels could exist within a partition (for example a partition containing processes running at different classification levels), between partitions on a processor or between partitions on different processors.

A systematic covert channel analysis is recommended for the Scenario C system. This is recommended because some users of the system are not cleared for all of the data, including users with non-US clearances, such as in the S//Rel cases. The system is also connected to external networks, which could introduce additional covert channels. Additionally, there may be covert channel analysis requirements levied on the components that make up the system.

Some covert channels cannot be eliminated due to real time constraints and the need for efficient access to shared resources. The certifier and accreditor of the system must ultimately decide on what level of risk is acceptable with regard to covert channels.

8.4.6   Privilege Mode Guidance

The minimal requirements for Scenario C for what should run in privilege mode are the Separation Kernel, any Architecture Support Package, and any Board Support Package. Since High Robustness is recommended for the SRTOS, additional code/applications should not be run in privilege mode. Any code/application in privilege mode has full, unrestricted access to all memory, resources, devices, etc, and can circumvent the security policy.

All code/applications, including runtime libraries and device drivers, running in privilege mode during operation should be High Robustness and are considered to be part of the SRTOS. Initialization and shutdown code or other code not executing during operation should also be High Robustness.

8.4.7   Protection Measures Guidance

Appropriate measures should be applied to ensure that unauthorized modifications to the system do not occur throughout its life cycle.

Procedures and security mechanisms are needed to ensure that any product with a role in enforcing the system's security policy has not been tampered with from its manufacturing/creation to its delivery (e.g. to the system integrator, application developer, or end user) and subsequent use. The integrity of the product must be protected during the initial delivery and any subsequent updates, and verified to ensure that the version used in the system matches the desired or intended manufacturer/vendor version.

Trusted delivery is used for the initial version distribution as well as for distribution of updates. Trusted delivery requires verification through procedures and/or tools that the version of the product used in the system and the desired or intended manufacturer/vendor version match. Electronic signature is a possible mechanism to use for trusted delivery of software. For hardware, shipment in containers that would show evidence of tampering is a possible mechanism. Incoming inspection could verify signatures on software and check for evidence of tampering with shipping containers.

There are several ways to mitigate the risk of integrating maliciously modified products. One such way is via a "blind buy." This is when the customer purchases a product using a pseudo-name to shield their identity from the vendor. There should also be consideration of the source of the product (offshore parts, etc.). Distribution and storage should also be taken into account.

After the system is delivered there is a risk that anyone with physical access to the system could modify and subvert the system. The unauthorized user must be prevented from maliciously altering the system. For example, an uncleared maintenance person could install a new product that had been maliciously modified. To mitigate this risk policy and procedures should control physical access to the system by anyone other than US persons with a clearance for all data that the system is approved to process. To detect inappropriate modification anti-tamper techniques such as tamper evident seals or other mechanisms are recommended. A person such as a maintainer may need to violate the anti-tamper in order to perform a needed function, and therefore must be cleared to the level of the system.

Because the lack of physical protection in Scenario C merits stricter protection measures, there are additional mechanisms recommended for protection. Some of these include anti-reverse engineering technology, methods of clearing or zeroizing memory containing sensitive data once tampering is detected, encryption of data storage (or data-at-rest), and data checksums for tamper detection.

8.4.8 Guidance for Similar Cases

Processor/Hardware #4 in this example system warrants additional guidance from that provided above. This hardware set contains partitions running at the same security level with the same recommendation for robustness, with the exception of the Inter-Processor Communication (4Z) partition. The Inter-Processor Communication (4Z) and SRTOS are recommended to be High Robustness assuming that they are maintaining separation of data at different security levels in a Scenario C environment. If however #4 did not require a network connection to the Switch then there would be no Inter-Processor Communication (4Z) partition with possible access to data at different security levels. In this case, Medium Robustness may be appropriate for the SRTOS. Consider a second case where all data passing through the Switch is appropriately encrypted and signed. In this case, Inter-Processor Communications (4Z) should only have access to U data (and encrypted S and S//Rel data). It may be reasonable in this case to use a Medium Robustness SRTOS (on only processor #4) and Inter-Processor Communication (4Z). However, since the Medium Robustness Inter-Processor Communication (4Z) will be able to communicate with High Robustness Inter-Processor Communication partitions the issue of the Medium Robustness partition trying to subvert the High Robustness partitions should be addressed.

This example system used data at U, S//Rel and S. If instead the data was at S//Rel, S, and TS (not SCI) the same guidance would apply. Some adjustments may be appropriate based on the trust that the US can place in the nations represented by S//Rel (and how well those nations are able to protect the S//Rel Coalition Network). Using the guidance provided is appropriate for cases where there is not a high degree of trust in the other nations.

If the data was at S and TS and involved only cleared US users and connections to US networks/systems at S and TS, then the guidance provided for Scenario A may be more appropriate.

If the data was at S and TS/SCI and involved only cleared US users and connections to US networks/systems at S and TS/SCI, then the guidance provided for Scenario A may be more appropriate. Note that DCID 6/3 requirements, likely at Protection Level 4, would also apply.

8.5   IA GUIDANCE FOR SCENARIO D

8.5.1   Description of Scenario D

As described in the Environment Scenario section of this report, Scenario D reflects a system having the general characteristics summarized below:

- Physical Security: Security provided by the physical environment of the system is considered high risk. For example, the system may be a tactical weapon system that faces a realistic probability of being overrun by an adversary, thus giving the adversary physical access to the system (or a portion of the overall system).

- Type of Users: The system has local users within the system that are cleared Secret and Top Secret/SCI and other users that are uncleared.

- Security Domain Levels: The system processes Unclassified, Secret, and Top Secret/SCI data on a single processor.

- Network Connectivity: The system is connected to significant external networks/systems providing large numbers of remote people and processes some degree of access to the system. For example, the system may be connected to the NIPRNet, which is connected to the Internet creating an "electronic pathway" for data to flow from anyone on the Internet into the system.

- Applications: The system has broad applications that are in wide use and have known vulnerabilities. An example is a commonly used word processor.

- Protocols and Data Types: The protocols and data types are considered broad. They are in wide use and have known vulnerabilities. An example of a broad protocol is the TCP/IP, which transfers messages. The data types are considered to be open format messages, such as the HTTP Web-based e-mail.

8.5.2   Analysis of Scenario D

Primary areas of risk for Scenario D include:

- Physical Security: There is a significant risk that people with physical access to the system may try to subvert the system. Lacking good physical security, an adversary has the opportunity to gain physical access, for example in an overrun situation.

- Type of Users: There is a significant insider risk posed by the user that is not cleared for Top Secret/SCI information processed by the system, in particular the uncleared user. In addition, non-US users pose a risk since they are not cleared for all information processed by the system.

- Security Domain Levels: The system processes data from the Unclassified to TS/SCI level. The value of the data is very high hence an adversary would be willing to apply significant resources towards compromising the data and unclassified processing within the system presents an exploitation opportunity for the adversary.

- Network Connectivity: There is a significant risk posed by the connection to the NIPRNet/Internet. Anyone on the Internet has the opportunity to attack the system. In addition, the connections to the SIPRNet and in particular JWICS greatly increase the risk since the consequence of a security breach could involve harm to SIPRNet and/or JWICS.

- Applications, Protocols and Data Types: Broadly used applications, protocols and open data types present a significant risk to the system. It is reasonable to expect that known vulnerabilities for these applications, protocols and data types are posted on the Internet and available to any adversary.

The most significant detail for Scenario D is that a single processor will process U through TS/SCI information and the U processing could be subverted by anyone on the Internet. This results in multiple cases where a single High Robustness component is responsible for protecting the most sensitive level of US information from the most capable of adversaries. In addition, compromise of the information could result from hardware failures, errors or omissions in integrating the components, and errors in implementing the system's security policy via multiple interdependent policy enforcement components.

8.5.3   Guidance for Scenario D

106

Due to the number of significant risks and the current limited ability to analyze complex systems it is highly recommended that developers refrain from implementing a system with similar characteristics and utilize an alternative system security architecture.

8.6 IA GUIDANCE FOR ALL SCENARIOS

8.6.1 Evaluation Guidance

Given that an evaluated product is available for implementation, the question often arises as to how much change or variation is permitted before additional evaluation is needed to maintain an evaluation rating such as a Common Criteria (CC) EAL.

An evaluated SRTOS is comprised of the Separation Kernel, the underlying board support and/or architectural support packages, any middleware that is running in privilege mode, and the hardware on which it is evaluated. Each component within the SRTOS needs to be evaluated to the same level of assurance. This section discusses the general question of re-evaluation, re-evaluation when changes are made to the SRTOS, and integrating a SRTOS with various individually evaluated components.

8.6.1.1 COMPONENT RE-EVALUATION

The question of re-evaluation is primarily a risk management/risk acceptance decision to be made by the system accreditor. Accreditors rely on the recommendations of the system certifier so it is very important that certification testing be thorough and complete. Changes to a certified and accredited system need to be examined to ensure the security policy is still enforced and to determine if individual components or parts of a system need to be re-evaluated.

The re-evaluation is the responsibility of the component or system developer. They need to ensure any changes to a component do not affect its evaluated assurance level and that integration of individually evaluated components results in the composition of a secure system.

The Common Criteria includes several assurance requirements that are relevant to re-evaluation. They include assurance level maintenance, configuration management and life cycle management requirements. Re-evaluation based on changes made to an individual component may be covered by the pertinent protection profile or security target.

Planned changes can result in unintended consequences so it may be necessary to independently confirm the developer's work. Independent review of changes performed by the system evaluators should determine that:

- The developers and/or system integrators performed tests to confirm correct and secure operation and function;

- Correct operation and function is confirmed through independent validation and verification (IV&V);

- Changes are documented and managed under a configuration management process in a manner that satisfies high robustness requirements;

- Developer/integrator and IV&V system documentation, configuration management documentation of changes, source code, test plans, procedures and results are available for independent review and analysis.

8.6.1.2 CHANGES TO THE SRTOS

The SKPP (U.S. Government Protection Profile for Separation Kernels in Environments Requiring High Robustness) provides some guidance for re-evaluating high robustness separation kernels. It includes an assurance requirement that calls for an "assurance maintenance plan." The plan must characterize the types of changes covered by the plan, provide a release schedule, and describe how the developer will analyze changes to the Target of Evaluation (TOE) to assure the EAL level is not affected. This requires that changes to the SRTOS must be planned, scheduled, and subjected to some level of analysis or evaluation. It would seem to follow that the requirement would apply to unplanned changes such as flaw remediation, discovery of new vulnerabilities, or changes to the operating environment to include the threat model.

8.6.1.3 USE OF EVALUATED SRTOS ON DIFFERENT HARDWARE

An evaluation of an SRTOS covers the board support package/architecture support package, the Separation Kernel, and any software running in privilege mode on a particular hardware platform or processor. While the evaluation includes the hardware on which the SRTOS runs, the hardware itself is not evaluated as a discrete component. In cases where system developers plan to implement an evaluated SRTOS on different hardware without any changes to the SRTOS, consider running penetration tests of the SRTOS on the new hardware. A full re-evaluation of the SRTOS is not necessary.

In cases where the SRTOS had to be changed to run on the new hardware, conduct an evaluation of the security functions affected by the changes and any other testing that is deemed appropriate to check for unintended consequences resulting from the changes. In many cases a ratings maintenance plan would exist and that plan would be followed.

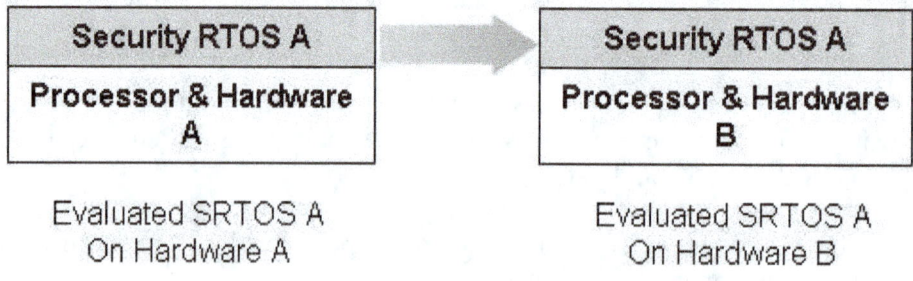

Figure 28: Evaluated SRTOS on New Hardware

8.6.1.4 USE OF EVALUATED APPLICATION ON ANOTHER SRTOS

If an application can be integrated onto another evaluated SRTOS without any changes to the application or SRTOS executable image, then a re-evaluation of the application would not be necessary. However a penetration test would be recommended since the SRTOS's processor/hardware would be changed. It's very unlikely that both application and SRTOS would have the same logic. They would probably have different logic, components, etc. which would give the need for testing. If the application changed, and it is security relevant, then testing would also be necessary.

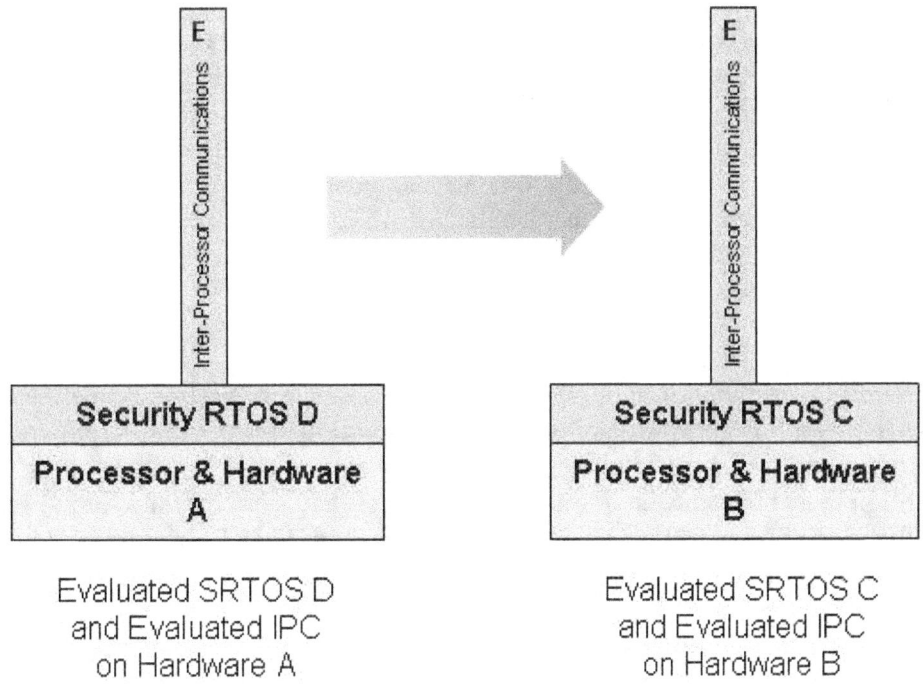

Figure 29: Evaluated Application an Another SRTOS

8.6.1.5 INTEGRATING INDIVIDUALLY EVALUATED COMPONENTS

In the case where individually evaluated components are integrated into a system, it is not necessary to re-evaluate each of the components in the context of the integrated system. It is important to understand how the evaluated pieces interoperate so the interfaces between and among the components should be analyzed. This can be performed under the normal certification and accreditation procedures. Under the DoD Information Technology Security Certification and Accreditation Process (DITSCAP), this would involve the phase four change management and compliance validation tasks. This includes repeating the appropriate tasks of phase two and phase three.

A review and analysis of the applicable security targets and protection profiles is necessary to look for gaps in the security provided by the individual components as they are integrated into a system. A gap analysis would identify security functions that need to be re-evaluated. From the gap analysis, develop a re-evaluation plan for approval by the system certifier.

8.6.2 Secure System Architecture Guidance

A secure system architecture is a system architecture that adequately addresses the IA threat to the system. It is often achieved through the sound application of Information Systems Security Engineering. Testing, analysis and other actions are typically used to ensure that the system is secure.

8.6.3 Partition Guidance

Each partition can contain multiple applications/code, often from different vendors. For example, the U Firewall (1C) partition from the example system for Scenario C would likely contain: a Network Interface Card (NIC) Device Driver to enable the partition to communicate with the physical network interface provided as part of the #1 Processor and Hardware; a Protocol Stack to allow the firewall application to exchange data with computers/devices on the NIPRNet via TCP/IP; and, an Application Proxy Firewall to provide proxies for applications running in other partitions (such as the Web browser in U User Browser Application (2F)) to protect those applications from potential attackers on the NIPRNet or Internet.

Careful consideration should be given to the number of partitions and the content of each. If only a few partitions are used then each will likely contain a significant number of functions and if any of the functions are security critical then all of the code in that partition must be evaluated to the assurance level that is appropriate for the security critical function. For example, consider the case where a Basic Robustness application needs to use a Medium Robustness device driver. If the device driver and application are placed in the same partition then all the software (device driver plus application) should be evaluated to Medium Robustness. If on the other hand the device driver is in one partition and the application in another then the device driver can be evaluated to Medium Robustness and the application to Basic Robustness, likely saving time and money. As illustrated here, it is important that the allocation of functions to partitions be done early in the design of the system. If, using the prior example, the application was intended to be Basic Robustness so the documentation, testing, etc, had been done to that level then it may be very disruptive to the program to go back and redo the application, documentation, testing, etc, to meet Medium Robustness.

While there are benefits to using multiple partitions to reduce evaluation cost and time there are also physical and complexity limitations on having too many partitions. The number of partitions (domains) is for the most part limited by amount of physical memory available. Also, depending on the motherboard architecture, the number of available partitions can vary because of the way the Memory Management Unit (MMU) works. An analysis should be performed to ensure that the performance and resource requirements of each partition could be satisfied when they are combined and share a single processor/computer. In addition, with large numbers of partitions on a processor the complexity of the information flow control policy increases greatly and consideration should be given to whether the complexity will exceed what can be understood and evaluated.

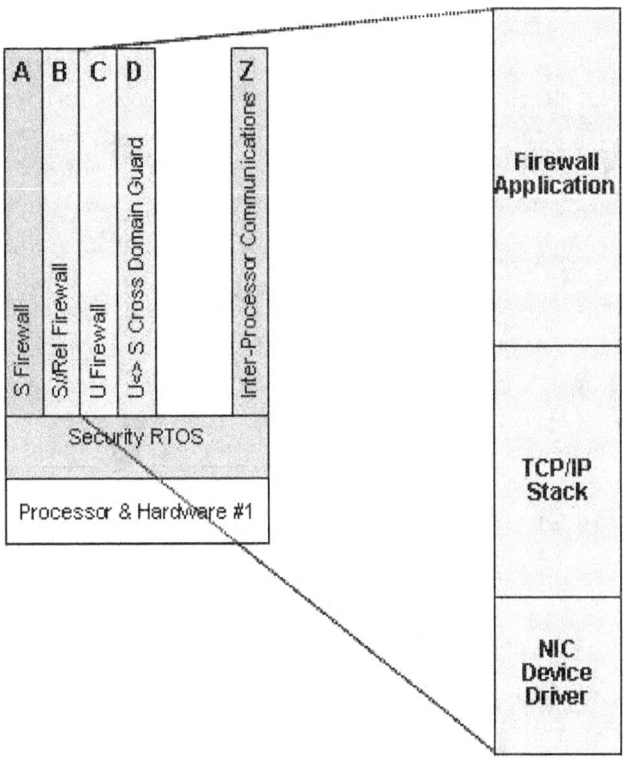

Figure 30: Partition Contents

8.6.4 Cache Guidance

Cache use should be consistent with that used during the SRTOS evaluation. For example, if L2 cache was disabled or not present during the SRTOS evaluation then L2 cache should not be used/enabled in a system implementing that SRTOS and hardware without adequate impact analysis and re-evaluation. If, however, the cache was enabled and the appropriate requirements were specified in the Security Target and evaluated, then the cache may be enabled. A primary concern with cache would be its use as a covert channel for possible communications between partitions. It however does not appear to be a concern that a partition would be able to gain access to information in the cache that was left there by another partition. An option to avoid a covert channel and any other opportunity for obtaining residual data from the cache would be to flush the cache during each context switch. This however could significantly affect performance, especially for large cache sizes.

8.6.5 Direct Memory Access Guidance

Direct Memory Access (DMA) can allow a peripheral/device to access memory directly, without the memory access going through the processor/ MMU and the SRTOS. In this case, the peripheral/device (such as a Network Interface Card) can circumvent the SRTOS and subvert the system, violating the system's security policy.

111

For this case it is recommended that any peripheral/device that would use DMA be evaluated to the same assurance level (Medium Robustness or High Robustness) as the SRTOS in that system. Ideally the evaluation would include conformance to an appropriate US Government Protection Profile. In many cases such a Protection Profile will not exist and a detailed understanding of the Security Target for the peripheral/device will be necessary to ensure the evaluation is adequate and that the peripheral/device can be trusted to enforce the system's security policy.

If a mechanism is used to ensure that memory access via DMA is restricted to specific addresses then it is possible that a device using DMA would only require evaluation to Basic Robustness. However, the mechanism that enforces the memory access restrictions via DMA should be evaluated at the same assurance level (Medium Robustness or High Robustness) as the SRTOS in the system.

8.6.6 Scheduling Guidance

It is important to ensure that security critical functions receive sufficient processor cycles. An analysis should be performed that demonstrates that this will hold true. Possible issues to consider are priority escalation, where a lower priority process can effectively deny resources to a higher priority process, and priority deadlock where two processes can effectively deny each other resources by each holding access to a resource required by the other. Many commercial priority-based scheduling solutions address these issues. One possible method is to use an ARINC-653 compliant scheduler that allocates a fixed number of processor cycles to each partition.

8.6.7 Inter-Processor Communications Guidance

In the scenarios described, Processor & Hardware #3 and #4 are connected via the Dedicated Bus and the U Comms Device Driver partitions. No significant security issues need to be addressed in this instance because the partitions are processing information at the same classification level and the information is transferred over a dedicated bus.

Another means for transferring information between processors is the Inter-Processor Communications (IPC) partition on each of the four processors (partitions 1Z, 2Z, 3Z, and 4Z) that provides for the flow of classified and unclassified information between processors. The parts of IPC are the IPC partition on the processors and the Ethernet Switch. When a processor wants to communicate with another processor, the message is sent from that processor's IPC partition to the other processor's IPC partition via the Ethernet switch.

The IPC must be capable of enforcing an information flow control policy that specifies explicitly what partitions on each processor are permitted to communicate with which partitions on another processor. If this capability does not exist, the system would run the risk of information classified at one level being sent to a partition at a different classification level. For example in the scenario depicted in Figure 31 below, the IPC partitions ensure that the information that flows from S Firewall (1A), a partition on processor one, only flows to partitions at the same classification level on processor two, in this case S User Application (2A), and not to a partition at another classification, such as U User Browser Application (2F) on processor two. Therefore, the policy should only permit partitions operating at the same classification (and releasability) level to communicate with each other and with multi-level partitions and permit multi-level partitions to communicate with each other. It is also recommended that both IPCs involved in the transfer of information between processors check the source and destination pairing against the policy. If it is not possible for both the sending and receiving IPCs to perform the policy check, then the IPC on the processor receiving the information should perform the policy check.

Implicit or explicit labeling could be used to enforce flow control. Implicit labeling takes place when the IPC takes some existing characteristic of data and uses it as the actual label, for instance using the IP address of the S Firewall (1A) partition as a distinguishing label. Explicit labeling takes place when the IPC adds a label to the data, for instance if the IPC partition on processor one (1Z) added a classification header field containing the label for Secret to the data packet going from S Firewall (1A) on processor one to S User Application (2A) on processor two.

The SRTOS and/or IPC should also include a means to ensure that a partition cannot spoof its identity so as to circumvent policy. Again, spoofing could run the risk of information classified at one level being sent to a partition at a different classification level. To prevent spoofing it is important that the IPC not rely solely on information provided by a partition, since that partition may spoof its information. For example, to prevent spoofing, the IPC may access certain information from the SRTOS to determine if the label or address being provided by a partition is legitimate for that partition.

Using implicit/explicit labels or having the IPC sign and/or encrypt packets could mitigate spoofing.

The Ethernet Switch could possibly modify the information flowing between IPC partitions. Modifying the information between the IPC partitions could lead to classified packets being sent to the wrong partition or information within the packets being corrupted (the labels or information within the packets being changed or the information being made unreadable). To mitigate this risk, the IPC partition could send signed and/or encrypted packets to ensure the confidentiality and integrity of the information flow. The IPC or an NSA-certified cryptographic device could perform signing and/or encryption. For example, Inter-Processor Communications (1Z) could sign and encrypt the data packets being sent from S Firewall (1A) and then pass the encrypted/signed data packet via the Ethernet Switch to Inter-Processor Communications (2Z) that would perform decryption and a signature check prior to passing the data packet to S User Application (2A). The Ethernet Switch is discussed in detail in the following Section 8.6.8.

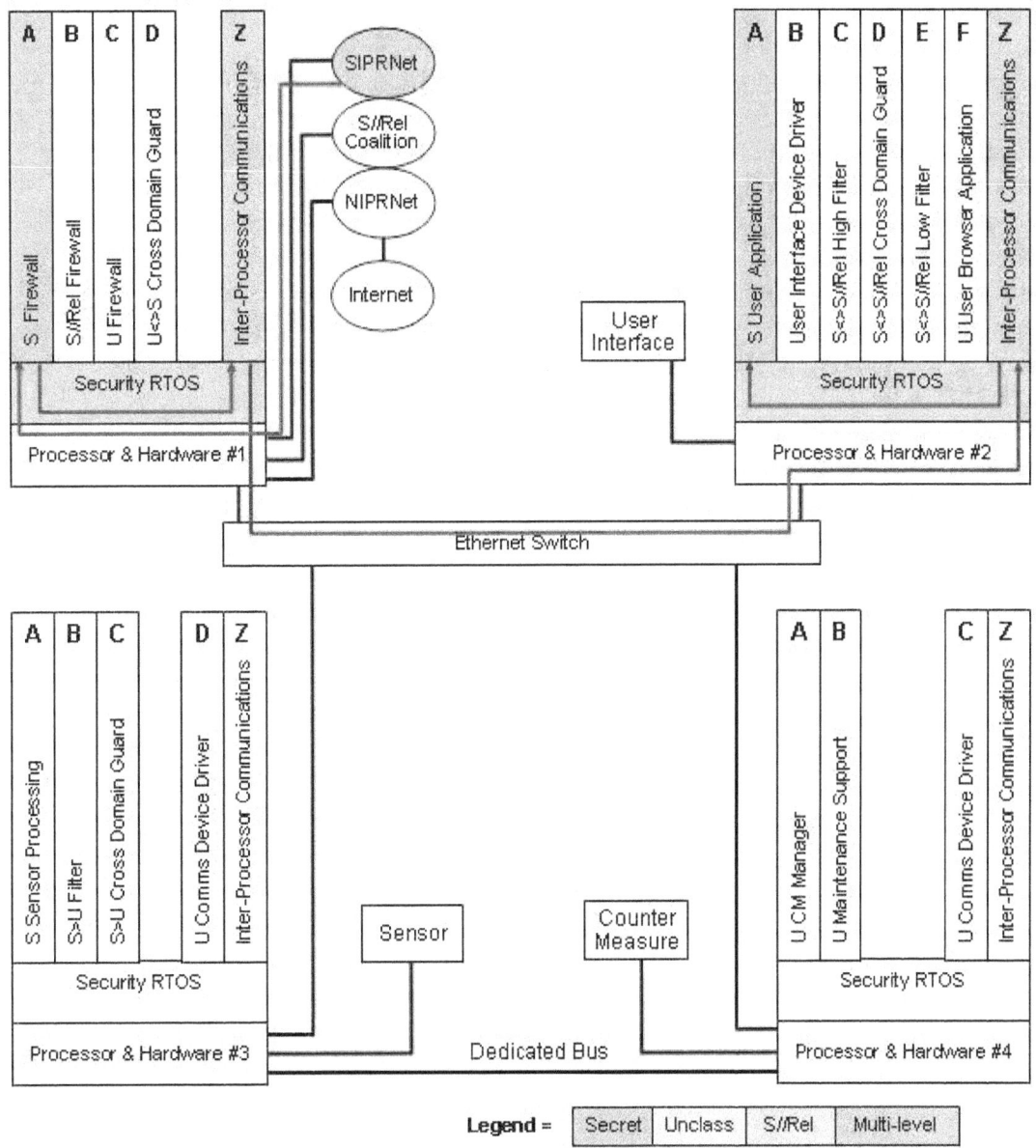

Figure 31: Scenario C SA Data from SIPRNet

8.6.8 Ethernet Switch Guidance

Within the scenarios described in this document, components can be identified that are responsible for enforcing a security policy. An example is the Inter-Processor Communications (1Z) partition/component that enforces an information flow control policy.

However, there is another type of component that is not responsible for enforcing a security policy, but could have the capability to circumvent the security policy. An example of this type of component is the Ethernet Switch. The Ethernet Switch provides an interconnection between the four Inter-Processor Communications partitions (1Z, 2Z, 3Z and 4Z). The information flows through the Ethernet Switch in packets. Some packets are unclassified (U), some are Secret (S), and some are Secret Releasable (S//Rel). The Inter-Processor Communications partitions enforce security policies ensuring that, for example, Secret packets of information cannot be sent from S User Application to U Firewall, and hence the unclassified NIPRNet (without having gone through a Cross Domain Guard to ensure the information being sent is unclassified). Assume that the Inter-Processor Communications uses addresses in the data packet to determine which partition is sending data to another. Suppose that the Ethernet Switch was malicious and could copy packets of information and modify the addressing within the packet (and compute a new, valid checksum as appropriate). If the Inter-Processor Communications partitions digitally signed each packet then the Ethernet Switch, even though potentially malicious, could not subvert the security policy. The Ethernet Switch could not subvert the security policy because if it did modify the addressing within a packet the modification would be detected by the Inter-Processor Communication partition that received the packet and determined that the digital signature was invalid (that the data had been modified in transit).

Consider a second case where the Inter-Processor Communication partition does not provide protection to the data so that any modification to a packet by the Ethernet Switch would be undetected by the Inter-Processor Communications partitions. For example (see Figure 32 below), if Secret information is supposed to be sent from S User Application (2A) to S Firewall (1A), and hence the SIPRNet, that information would flow through Inter-Processor Communications (2Z), the Ethernet Switch, and Inter-Processor Communications (1Z). Suppose the Ethernet Switch were to make a copy of the Secret packet and change the addressing to reflect that the packet was being sent from U User Browser Application (2F) to U Firewall (1C) and hence the NIPRNet and Internet, and then pass that copied packet to Inter-Processor Communications (1Z). Inter-Processor Communications (1Z) would apply its security policy appropriately, but since the information it is using to enforce the security policy has been modified an unfortunate decision will be made to pass the packet to U Firewall (1C).

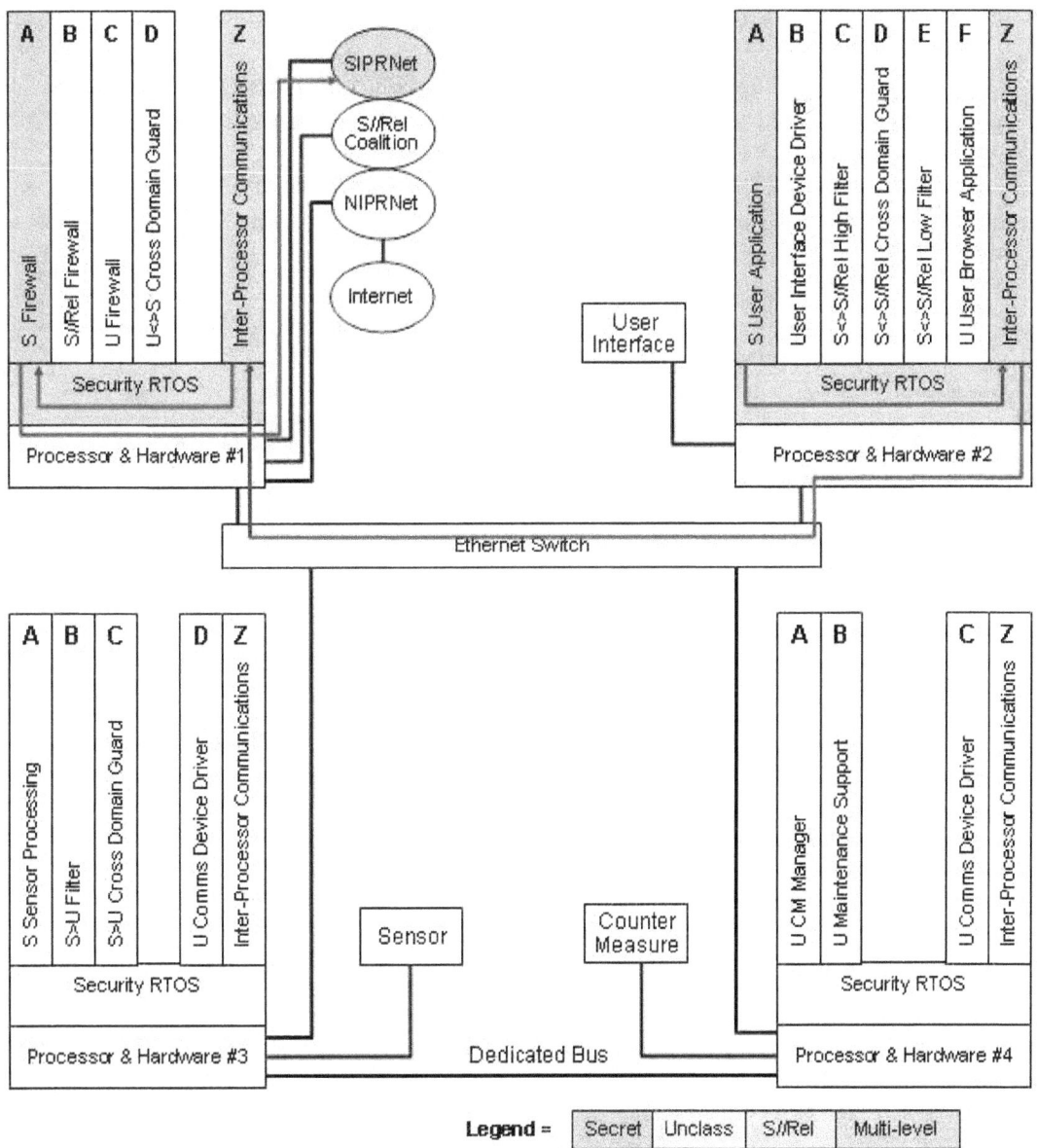

Figure 32: Scenario C Ethernet Switch Usage

In situations such as this the first step should be a thorough analysis to determine if the component has the actual capability necessary to subvert the security policy. In the case of the Ethernet Switch it is possible that it is a hardware device that can only examine data within a packet to determine which interface/port to which to pass the packet. If that is the case then that Ethernet Switch component can be purchased and used since it lacks the necessary capability that could be used to breach the security policy.

117

It is also possible that the Ethernet Switch is comprised of hardware and software and that the software is fixed and cannot be changed without physical access. It may still be possible to do a thorough analysis of the design to determine if the component, as designed, has the actual capability necessary to subvert the security policy.

A third possibility is that the Ethernet Switch is hardware and software and it is possible to provide software updates to the Ethernet Switch, but only via a specific management port. Analysis would need to include the capabilities of the Ethernet Switch itself as well whether the system uses the management port, what has access to that port, etc.

If the Ethernet Switch is hardware and software and it is possible to provide software updates to the Ethernet Switch via any interface/port then the analysis must focus on what has access to any of the ports and what confidence exists that those components will not modify the Ethernet Switch causing it to copy and modify packets and consequently breach the security policy.

While this guidance applies to the Ethernet Switch component in the scenarios described in this document an analysis of a system should be done to identify components that while not responsible for enforcing a security policy can subvert the security policy. Since much of the security focus is on the components enforcing the security policy it is feasible for these other types of components to exist within a system not receive much attention and consequently allow an adversary to subvert the system.

8.6.9   Device Guidance

When accessing a device from within a partition there are typically two components involved, a device driver and a peripheral/device. From the example systems described previously, peripherals would include the GPS Receiver, Sensor, Data Module, User Interface, Dedicated Bus, and Countermeasure. Device drivers would include the U Comms Device Driver, User Interface Device Driver, and Data Module Device Driver. Other device drivers are contained within partitions such as S Sensor Processing, U CM Manager, and others.

In some cases a device driver, the partition(s) that interface with the device driver, and the peripheral/device are at the same classification level, also referred to as a single-level device driver and peripheral/device. An example of this is the S User Interface Device Driver that interfaces to the S User Application partition and the User Interface peripheral/device in the example system for Scenario A.

In a second case a device driver may interface to multiple partitions each of which is in a different security domain. An example of this is the User Interface Device Driver in the example system for Scenario C that interfaces with both the S User Application and the U User Browser Application. In this case it is a multi-level device driver that must control the flow of information to and from the U and S partitions, ensuring that only unclassified information is provided to the U User Browser Application. Since the peripheral/device is responsible for enforcing the system's security policy in this case, the multi-level device driver has cross domain guard characteristics and should satisfy similar requirements. The multi-level device driver should not be able to be spoofed by a partition (a partition claiming to be another partition) and it should be able to handle/label data being received from and sent to the partitions appropriately. In this case it is the multi-level device driver's responsibility to ensure that the peripheral/device cannot, and cannot be used to, violate the system's security policy.

In a third case the peripheral/device may be the multi-level component accessed/shared by two or more device drivers and associated partitions operating at different security levels. There is no example of this case in the example systems. In this case it is the peripheral's responsibility to enforce the system's security policy. For example, a peripheral might be designed to accept classified data, process it, and return a result and then purge itself (perhaps by restarting itself) such that it could then accept unclassified data and process it. The multi-level peripheral should meet the robustness specified in the example systems for a multi-level device driver. The actual device drivers in this case should meet the robustness specified in the example systems for a single-level device driver.

Device drivers should not be run in privilege mode if possible. Even a device driver that is not in privilege mode (that runs in a partition) will often require a minimal piece of code to run in privilege mode. By minimizing the code in privilege mode possible re-evaluation of the SRTOS (which includes all code in privilege mode) is easier and less costly.

8.6.10 Static/Dynamic Guidance

Static/dynamic refer to the ability to make modifications to the system while in operation. Typically, changes to embedded systems do not take affect until the system is restarted. In some systems it may be necessary to have the capability to change the resources allocated to a partition (assign it more or less memory or processor cycles) and/or to change the information flow control policy. A dynamic SRTOS is one that includes the capability to make these types of changes while in operation given some command/stimulus from a partition or interface. If possible, it is recommended that the system architecture avoid this situation. This can sometimes be accomplished by pre-placing alternative configurations and implementing a secure process for moving from one configuration to another.

It is recommended that a dynamic SRTOS only be used if both it and the application directing the SRTOS changes have been evaluated to the same assurance level and both are found to do exactly what they are designed to do and nothing more. All of the possible states/changes that the SRTOS can assume should be pretested and shown to be properly constructed. Under these circumstances:

1. An information flow security policy change can be made while the SRTOS is in operation.

2. A change in the assignment of memory can be made while the SRTOS is in operation.

3. A change in the assignment of processor cycles can be made while the SRTOS is in operation.

The second item should require that the SRTOS clear any memory prior to reassigning it. The third item assumes the use of a hard/rigid partition scheduler such as an ARINC-653 scheduler.

It should be noted that a static machine is a simpler machine than a dynamic machine. Proofs of dynamic systems are therefore more difficult. Simplicity, in itself, promotes security. Fewer mistakes in design, implementation and configuration are likely to be made. Although the SKPP allows dynamic configuration changes, developers are cautioned that they must be able to demonstrate secure state following a configuration change.

8.6.11 Trusted Initialization Guidance

The focus of trusted initialization is to ensure that the system reaches the intended/predicted secure state when it is initialized (at power up or restart).

In some cases the SRTOS itself is responsible for the system reaching its initial state. It often relies on appropriate system parameters set in some initialization file. In this case, an analysis should be performed to determine if there is any way that the SRTOS code or the initialization file/data could be altered inappropriately during operation such that at the next power-up or restart the system would reach a subverted initial state. In addition, mechanisms may need to be included to verify that the SRTOS code and/or initialization file/data has not been altered by an unauthorized action. The analysis and checking mechanisms should also be applied to any component (and its initialization data) for which Medium or High Robustness is recommended, and consideration should be given to applying the analysis and checking mechanisms to all components. In essence, it must be known that a secure initial processing state has been reached, and that the secure state is maintained thereafter.

In other cases special initialization/boot code may be responsible for starting the SRTOS. For example, the code may be needed to access a peripheral/device that stores the SRTOS code. In this case the same analysis and checking mechanisms described above should be applied to this initialization/boot code to ensure that it cannot cause the system to initialize in a subverted state. In some distributed architectures, a series of initial states may be needed.

Once running, the SRTOS will create the partitions. The SRTOS should ensure that any memory or other resources assigned to a partition are cleared/sanitized prior to being assigned. The parameters and code for each partition are typically stored in non-volatile memory. The system should ensure that the parameters and code for partition B couldn't be accessed or modified by partition A that may already be running. This is often accomplished by requiring a physical action (such as moving a hardware strap) to enable changes to non-volatile memory. If this is not practical, for example the system must be capable of receiving updated versions of partition B to be used at next restart, then the software that is capable of changing the contents of non-volatile memory should be evaluated to the same robustness level as the SRTOS in the system. This capability may be a function of the SRTOS and be in privilege mode, but it will more often be a function running in a partition. This function should include a mechanism for verifying that the updated parameters/code came from a legitimate source and that the information has not been altered since it left the source.

8.6.12 System Level Robustness

When these components are implemented in a secure system architecture in an appropriate manner the system can be adequately secured against the threat it faces. The system however cannot be described as a High Robustness system (or Medium or Basic). The system, as a composition of components, undergoes a certification and accreditation process to determine if it is acceptable from a security perspective. The certification and accreditation process examines evidence concerning the verification and validation of the system, identifies residual risk, and makes a determination whether that residual risk is acceptable. From a system level perspective the system is either acceptable or unacceptable once all factors have been considered by the appropriate authorities.

9 POLICIES, REGULATIONS, ETC.

This section will explore applicability and interpretation of key policies relative to the defined environment scenarios.

9.1 NSTISSP 11

The National Security Telecommunications and Information Systems Security Policy (NSTISSP) 11, National Policy Governing the Acquisition of Information Assurance (IA) and IA-Enabled Information Technology (IT) Products, establishes requirements for the acquisition and appropriate implementation of evaluated or validated Government Off-The-Shelf (GOTS) or COTS IA and IA-enabled IT products in National Security Systems. Embedded systems addressed by this document are assumed to process classified data and therefore are National Security Systems. The embedded systems will likely include multiple components. Some of those components will be responsible for enforcing the system's security policy. At the very least this would include the SRTOS. The components with a role in enforcing the system's security policy should be considered to be IA or IA-enabled products and therefore should comply with NSTISSP 11. The IASE Web site, http://iase.disa.mil, contains a link to the most recent Frequently Asked Questions concerning NSTISSP 11.

For COTS IA or IA-enabled products that are evaluated under the NIAP (National Information Assurance Partnership) the product is evaluated and validated against a Security Target (ST), which often conforms to a PP. The NIAP program is described below:

The National Institute of Standards and Technology (NIST) and the National Security Agency (NSA) have established a program under the National Information Assurance Partnership (NIAP) to evaluate IT product conformance to international standards. The program, officially known as the NIAP Common Criteria Evaluation and Validation Scheme for IT Security (CCEVS) is a partnership between the public and private sectors. This program is being implemented to help consumers select commercial off-the-shelf information technology (IT) products that meet their security requirements and to help manufacturers of those products gain acceptance in the global marketplace.

A list of final and draft Protection Profiles can be found at the NIAP Web site: http://niap.nist.gov. A partial list of potentially relevant protection profiles would include:

DRAFT

- Operating System (OS) - Application Platform

- US Government Protection Profile Separation Kernels in Environments Requiring for High Robustness Environments

- Middleware-Common Object Request Broker Architecture (CORBA)

122

- Middleware-Partitioning Communications System

VALIDATED

- Protection Profile for Multilevel Operating System in Environments Requiring Medium Robustness

9.2 DODI 8500.2

The SRTOS-based embedded system should comply with the IA controls of Department of Defense Instruction (DODI) 8500.2, Information Assurance Implementation. DODI 8500.2 provides guidance for carrying out policy, designating roles and responsibilities, and laying down procedures for applying protection to the DoD information systems and networks.

Two factors go into choosing the correct IA controls that apply to the SRTOS-based embedded system.

The first factor is the Mission Assurance Category (MAC). The MAC category addresses integrity and availability of information that is vital to the system's mission. MAC categories range from I to III, with I providing the most thorough protection.

The other factor that aids in choosing the proper IA control is the confidentiality level of the system. The confidentiality level is used to describe the classification and sensitivity of information on the system. The three levels of this factor are classified, sensitive, and public.

This document assumes that the SRTOS-based embedded systems are MAC I and are processing classified information. Many of the IA controls will apply to the SRTOS-based embedded systems in this document. Some IA controls will apply more than others, while other IA controls will have to be modified, tailored, or omitted.

9.3 DCID 6/3

Director of Central Intelligence Directive (DCID) 6/3, Protecting Sensitive Compartmented Information Within Information Systems, establishes the security policies and procedures for storing, processing, and communicating classified intelligence information in information systems. For the purposes of DCID 6/3, "intelligence information" refers to Sensitive Compartmented Information and special access programs for intelligence under the purview of the Director of National Intelligence (DNI). An "information system" is any telecommunications and/or computer related equipment or interconnected system or subsystems of equipment that is used in the acquisition, storage, manipulation, management, movement, control, display, switching, interchange, transmission, or reception of voice and/or data; it includes software, firmware and hardware.

An SRTOS-based embedded system should comply with DCID 6/3 if the information stored, processed or communicated in a scenario satisfies the above definition for "classified intelligence information".

9.4   INFORMATION ASSURANCE TECHNICAL FRAMEWORK

The objectives of the Information Assurance Technical Framework (IATF) include raising the awareness of IA technologies, presenting the IA needs of information system (IS) users, providing guidance for solving IA issues, and highlighting gaps between current IA capabilities and needs. When developing an effective IA posture, the four below components of the Defense-In-Depth strategy need to be addressed by SRTOS-based embedded systems.

1. **Defend the Network Infrastructure**: Here the IATF describes the types of network traffic-users, control, and management--- and the basic requirements to ensure that network services remain both available and secure.

2. **Defend the Enclave Boundary**: Here the IATF focuses on effective control and monitoring of the data flows into and out of the enclave. Effective control measures include firewalls, guards, Virtual Private Networks (VPN), and identification and authentication access and control for remote users. Effective monitoring mechanisms include network-based intrusion detection systems (IDS), vulnerability scanners, and virus detectors. These mechanisms work alone, and in concert within each other to provide defenses for those systems within the enclave.

3. **Defend the Computing Environment**: The computing environment includes the end-user workstation both desktop and laptop to include peripheral devices. Servers include application, network, Web, file, and internal communication servers. A fundamental tenet of the Defense-in-Depth strategy is preventing cyber attacks from penetrating networks and compromising the confidentiality, integrity, and availability of the computing environment information. Also addressed are host-based sensors, including those that operate in near real time as well as those that operate off-line.

4. **Support the System Infrastructure**: Here the IATF addresses two supporting infrastructure entities: Key Management Infrastructure (KMI)/Public Key Infrastructure (PKI) and Detect and Respond. KMI/PKI focuses on the technologies, services, and processes used to manage public key certificates and symmetric cryptography. The discussion concludes with recommendations for the features needed to achieve the three global information grid-defined assurance levels: basic, medium and high.

Two important processes are included in the IATF. These processes are the Systems Engineering (SE) process and the ISSE process. The ISSE process is presented as a natural extension of the systems engineering process. The two process share common elements: discovering needs; defining system functionality; designing system elements; producing and installing the system and assessing the effectiveness of the system. Other elements would include systems acquisition, risk management, certification and accreditation and life cycle support processes.

The IATF provides the background for detailed technical discussions. It presents general discussions of the principles for determining appropriate technical security countermeasures to include detailed descriptions of threats, including attacker motivations, information security services, and appropriate security technologies. Decisions from these discussions form the basis for developing appropriate technical countermeasures for the identified threats, based on the value of information.

10 ACRONYMS

ACRONYM	DEFINITION
ASCII	American Standard Code for Information Interchange
ASP	Architecture Support Package
BSP	Board Support Package
CC	Common Criteria
CCEVS	Common Criteria Evaluation and Validation Scheme
CDS	Cross Domain Solutions
CJCSM	Chairman of the Joint Chiefs of Staff Manual
CM	Countermeasure
CNSS	The Committee for National Security Systems
CORBA	Common Object Request Broker Architecture
COTS	Commercial Off-The-Shelf
CPU	Central Processing Unit
DCID	Director of Central Intelligence Directive
DICAST	Defense Intelligence Communication Accreditation Support Team
DISN	Defense Information Support Network
DITSCAP	DoD Information Technology Security Certification and Accreditation Process
DMA	Direct Memory Access
DNI	Director of National Intelligence
DoD	Department of Defense
DODD	Department of Defense Directive
DODI	Department of Defense Instruction
DSAWG	DISN Security Accreditation Working Group
EAL	Evaluated Assurance Level
F/A	Fighter/Attack
FAA	Federal Aviation Administration
FCS	Future Combat Systems
GOTS	Government Off-The-Shelf
GPS	Global Positioning System
HTTP	Hypertext Transfer Protocol
IA	Information Assurance
IAD	Information Assurance Directorate
IATF	Information Assurance Technical Framework
IDS	Intrusion Detection System
IPC	Inter-Processor Communications
IS	Information System
ISSE	Information System Security Engineer
IT	Information Technology

ACRONYM	DEFINITION
IV&V	Independent Validation and Verification
JWICS	Joint Worldwide Intelligence Communications System
KMI	Key Management Infrastructure
MAC	Mission Assurance Category
MMU	Memory Management Unit
NIAP	National Information Assurance Program
NIC	Network Interface Card
NIPRNet	Non-Classified Internet Protocol Router Network
NIST	National Institute of Standards and Technology
NSA	National Security Agency
NSTISSP	National Security Telecommunications and Information Systems Security Policy
OS	Operating System
PC	Personal Computer
PKI	Public Key Infrastructure
PP	Protection Profile
RTOS	Real-Time Operating System
S	Secret
S//Rel	Secret Coalition Network
SA	Situational Awareness
SAP	Special Access Program
SAR	Special Access Required
SCI	Sensitive Compartmented Information
SE	Systems Engineering
SECNET	Secure Network
SIPRNet	Secret Internet Protocol Router Network
SKPP	Separation Kernel Protection Profile
SMP	Symmetric Multi-Processing
SRTOS	Security Real-Time Operating System
ST	Security Target
TCP/IP	Transmission Control Protocol/Internet Protocol
TOE	Target of Evaluation
TS	Top Secret
TS//Rel	Top Secret//Releasable
U	Unclassified
UK	United Kingdom
US	United States
VPN	Virtual Private Network

11 FUTURE TOPICS

As described in the Assumptions and Constraints section, the guidance provided assumes the SRTOS is running on a single core processor. However multi-core processors are becoming increasingly popular and as prices decrease they will be used in embedded systems. A follow-on effort will be necessary to determine what additions and/or changes to this document are necessary to provide IA guidance for embedded systems in which the SRTOS is running on a multi-core processor.